PENGUIN PASSNOTES

The Adventures of Huckleberry Finn

Iona McGregor was educated at Bristol University and worked until recently as a teacher in Edinburgh. She has published several historical novels and educational books for young people.

PENGUIN PASSNOTES

MARK TWAIN
The Adventures of Huckleberry Finn

IONA McGREGOR
ADVISORY EDITOR: S. H. COOTE M.A., PH.D

PENGUIN BOOKS

PENGUIN BOOKS

Published by the Penguin Group
27 Wrights Lane, London W8 5TZ, England
Viking Penguin Inc., 40 West 23rd Street, New York, New York 10010, USA
Penguin Books Australia Ltd, Ringwood, Victoria, Australia
Penguin Books Canada Ltd, 2801 John Street, Markham, Ontario, Canada L3R 1B4
Penguin Books (NZ) Ltd, 182–190 Wairau Road, Auckland 10, New Zealand

Penguin Books Ltd, Registered Offices: Harmondsworth, Middlesex, England

First published 1988

Copyright © Iona McGregor, 1988
All rights reserved

Made and printed in Great Britain by
Richard Clay Ltd, Bungay, Suffolk
Filmset in Monophoto Ehrhardt

Except in the United States of America, this book is sold subject
to the condition that it shall not, by way of trade or otherwise, be lent,
re-sold, hired out, or otherwise circulated without the
publisher's prior consent in any form of binding or cover other than
that in which it is published and without a similar condition
including this condition being imposed on the subsequent purchaser

Contents

To the Student vii
Introduction: Mark Twain and *The Adventures of
    Huckleberry Finn* 1
Synopsis of *The Adventures of Huckleberry Finn* 6
An Account of the Plot 19
Characters 63
Commentary 75
Glossary 95
Discussion Topics and Examination Questions 99

To the Student

This book is designed to help you with your O-level, CSE or GCSE English Literature examinations. It contains a synopsis of the novel, a glossary of the more unfamiliar words and phrases, and a commentary on some of the issues raised by the text. An account of the writer's life is also included for background.

Page references in parentheses refer to the Penguin edition of Mark Twain's *The Adventures of Huckleberry Finn*.

When you use this book, remember that it is no more than an aid to your study. It will help you find passages quickly and perhaps give you some ideas for essays. But remember also: *This book is not a substitute for reading the novel, and it is your knowledge and your response that matter*. These are the things that the examiners are looking for, and they are also the things that will give you the most pleasure. Show your knowledge and appreciation to the examiner, and show them clearly.

Introduction: Mark Twain and The Adventures of Huckleberry Finn

Mark Twain was the pen-name adopted by Samuel Langhorne Clemens (1835–1910), an American printer, journalist and steamboat pilot who became the most famous humorous writer of his day.

Samuel Clemens grew up in Hannibal, Missouri, in the southwestern United States. His boyhood there, and his experiences as a Mississippi pilot, lie behind his two best-known works, *The Adventures of Tom Sawyer* (1876) and *The Adventures of Huckleberry Finn* (1884–5). The way Twain used this material was greatly influenced by his attitudes to the American society of his day and by the contradictory elements in his own life. So it is necessary to know something about these to understand *The Adventures of Huckleberry Finn*.

The Clemens family were typical of an America still in the frontier-pushing, melting-pot stage of its development. They moved restlessly from place to place, taking up one kind of work after another; they speculated in land and a great variety of business enterprises and inventions, usually with no luck. Alongside Mark Twain's success as a writer, this family pattern pursued him to the end of his life.

In 1847 Samuel's father – lawyer, judge, farmer, storekeeper, trader – died and left his family in poverty. Samuel became an apprentice printer and also wrote pieces for a local newspaper. He then began to travel round the States as a master printer, but in 1857 decided to look for gold in South America. In New Orleans, he changed his mind and trained to be a pilot on the Mississippi.

This career, which Twain looked back to with wistful regret, was terminated by the American Civil War (1861–5). After a fortnight in the Confederate army, Samuel, sick of military life, went with his brother Orion to Nevada, hoping for quick wealth from the silver mines. His hopes were dashed and Samuel returned to Virginia City to work as a journalist. In 1863 he published his first piece of comic writing under the name of 'Mark Twain', a memory of his river days: the cries of 'Mark one', 'Mark twain', 'Mark three', etc. indicated the depth of water under the huge Mississippi steamboats.

Mark Twain turned to full-time journalism, basing himself in San Francisco. His life in the 'sub-culture of reporters, entertainers, actors, theater managers, acrobats, ladies of the chorus, prospectors, and short-term promoters' (Justin Kaplan, *Mr Clemens and Mark Twain*) broadened his scope as a writer, but was later to set up great strains when he tried to root himself in conventional East Coast society.

In 1865 Twain had a short story published in the New York *Saturday Press* – 'Jim Smiley and His Jumping Frog'. The piece was reprinted all over the States. His success made Twain decide to go to New York, the largest city in the United States, and now its centre for finance, journalism and publishing. There he also became drawn into the 'lyceum circuit'. This was the system of lecture tours organized by agencies that sent out authors and speakers all over the United States – a habit still popular there today. Mark Twain found that his talent for entertaining friends with amusing stories could be perfected into bringing him a hundred dollars a night; this was the start of the close links between the written and spoken word which is such a feature of Twain's work, as well as his reworking of the same material to be used in different ways.

In 1867 a Californian newspaper paid for him to join a five-month cruise to Europe and the Middle East, organized by Henry Ward Beecher, minister of Plymouth Church in Brooklyn. Twain was to report back in a series of letters. The other passengers were drawn mostly from the new American middle class and Twain's contact with them set up a pattern that was to mould the rest of his life. On the one hand, he was infuriated by what he saw as their pious and stifling respectability; but part of his nature longed to be accepted by them and share their stable and financially comfortable background. They were in fact representative of the people to whom most of this writing would be addressed.

On board the *Quaker City* he became very friendly with Mary Fairbanks, who was reporting on the cruise for the Cleveland *Herald*, edited by her husband. 'The most ... cultivated lady on the ship', Twain wrote to his family. 'She sewed my buttons on ... lectured me awfully ... and cured me of several bad habits.' Mrs Fairbanks also edited out of Twain's own reports anything she thought too vulgar or irreverent and he meekly accepted her judgement.

This friendship prefigured the 'sivilizing' role later taken by Olivia Langdon, the woman Twain married. Secure domesticity had a great appeal for Twain and the conflict between this and his rumbustious West Coast background emerges in the choice between freedom and civilization, which forms one of the major themes of his masterpiece, *The Adventures of Huckleberry Finn*.

The letters Twain wrote from the *Quaker City* were transformed into *The Innocents Abroad*, published in 1869. It was a very much padded account of the cruise, in which Twain poses as an incredibly naive American tourist describing the mishaps that overtook him and his fellow-passengers. Skilfully, he also manages to 'debunk' some of the pretentious, reverent attitude towards the culture the tourists felt obliged to admire. The book was a great success, selling sixty thousand copies within a year of its publication.

On the ship, Twain had met Charles Langdon, a young man from a wealthy New York State family, who introduced him to his sister Olivia. It took Twain three years to persuade the Langdons – and Olivia herself – that he would be a suitable husband for her, but in 1870 they eventually married and settled down in Hartford, Connecticut, about one hundred miles from both New York and Boston.

Here Mark Twain produced his best work. He lived very extravagantly, but despite this and his involvement in disastrous speculations and investments, he managed to meet his debts through lecture tours and his success as a writer. After 1891, he spent most of his time in Europe, visiting the States only to see to his business interests. In 1894 he suffered a serious bankruptcy, although once more he was able to recover from his debts by making a mammoth lecture tour.

Mark Twain had a high reputation in Europe but the East Coast literary establishment of his own country was slow to acknowledge his status as a man of letters. He was regarded as a brilliant satirist and exponent of frontier humour but not as a serious writer. Towards the end of his life, this began to change: his literary reputation was established and the American universities conferred honorary degrees on him.

His last years were saddened by the death of his wife and two of his three daughters. (His only son died in early childhood.) Twain himself died in 1910.

Twain's later works show a deepening pessimism and disgust with human nature, both in the individual and in society. Some of these darker strands already appear in *The Adventures of Huckleberry Finn*.

The novel centres round the story of a double bid for freedom: Huckleberry Finn, fleeing from his drunken father and the pressures of small-town society, rides down the Mississippi on a raft with Jim, an escaped Negro slave.

The book began as a proposed sequel to *The Adventures of Tom Sawyer*. Twain was already thinking about it in 1874, before the first book was finished, and a great many characters appear in both. Both stories are set in the forties, the time of Twain's boyhood, and *The Adventures of Huckleberry Finn* begins in 'St Petersburg' (Hannibal) which is also the setting for the whole of *The Adventures of Tom Sawyer*.

However, the two books are entirely different in purpose and outlook. It is true, of course, that *The Adventures of Tom Sawyer* is not merely a child's adventure story. Twain, as the narrator, deliberately contrasts the freshness and spontaneity of his child characters with the devitalized and often hypocritical adults; yet the satire is gentle, and it is made obvious that the children's freedom to rebel and behave outrageously depends on the firm protection of the adult world. In the end even the social outcast, Huck Finn, acquires security by being adopted by a kindly widow.

In *The Adventures of Huckleberry Finn*, Twain was working over his boyhood at a much deeper level and the themes that surface make it a much more complex book. Difficulties in dealing with these made Twain put the book aside in 1876 after writing the first sixteen chapers at immense speed. He worked at it sporadically over the next seven years.

The story is told by Huck himself, in south-western dialect. This in itself was a shock to the first readers. Dialect was extensively used by American writers but only within certain limits. No one had tried to write a story of this length in dialect and, above all, no one had used it to cover such a panoramic range of material as Mark Twain introduces into Huck's voyage down the Mississippi.

Modern readers on this side of the Atlantic have an advantage denied to the book's first European audience: much American usage has now passed into standard English; and from American cinema and TV films we are familiar with the sound of American voices. As you read *The Adventures of Huckleberry Finn*, try to *hear* the words, spoken in a drawling Southern accent: you will find that after a time the dialect will not cause any difficulty. Words that are totally different have been put into the Glossary (p. 95). Further help is given in the section of the Commentary headed 'Language' (p. 89).

The novel quickly became popular with the general public but the literary establishment were not so happy with it, nor those who felt that Huck's subversive social attitudes set a bad example. The library committee of Concord, Massachusetts, excluded it from the shelves. (Predictably, as with other books that have been banned, this only increased its fame.) By unfavourable critics it was described as 'flat', 'coarse', full of 'harmful morality', etc. However, it received some good reviews in newspapers even at its first appearance. After the tide began to turn in its favour, there was no more disagreement about the stature of the book, now unanimously regarded as a modern classic. The best-known comment about it is Ernest Hemingway's: 'All modern American literature comes from one book by Mark Twain called *Huckleberry Finn* ... There was nothing before. There has been nothing as good since.'

Nevertheless, there has been disagreement among critics about the purpose of the book and puzzlement over the final eleven chapters. About a hundred articles and books have been written about *The Adventures of Huckleberry Finn* since it first appeared, many of them contradicting each other. The following notes will try to guide you towards an understanding of the main themes and to the questions you should ask yourself when studying the book. In the end, however, you must make up your mind for yourself. Like all great works of literature, *The Adventures of Huckleberry Finn* has many layers of meaning and can be interpreted in many ways.

Synopsis of
The Adventures of Huckleberry Finn

The story is prefaced by a 'Notice' which sets the humorous tone of the opening chapters. There is also an 'Explanatory' paragraph about the dialects used in the novel.

CHAPTER 1, pp. 49–52

The story is set in the 1840s, in the Mississippi River valley, before the American Civil War. The hero and narrator, Huckleberry Finn, introduces himself and refers to previous exploits in *The Adventures of Tom Sawyer*. Since then, he has 'lit out' to avoid Widow Douglas's efforts to 'sivilize' him; but he has been lured back by the promise of joining Tom Sawyer's band of robbers (p. 49). Huck describes how Mrs Douglas and her sister, Miss Watson, try to teach him table manners, correct spelling and bible stories. After family prayers, Huck goes up to his room and feels very depressed. He hears Tom Sawyer's signal outside and climbs out of the window to join him.

CHAPTER 2, pp. 53–9

As they sneak out of the garden, the boys are overheard by Miss Watson's slave, Jim, on whom Tom plays a trick. The 'gang' take a skiff downstream to a cave in the hillside. Tom explains the rules of the robber-band – taken from adventure stories. Huck returns home with his new clothes 'all greased up and clayey' (p. 59).

CHAPTER 3, pp. 60–64

Miss Watson tries to teach Huck to pray. A man is found drowned in the river and mistakenly thought to be Pap, Huck's father. Huck becomes disillusioned with the gang's tame activities.

CHAPTER 4, pp. 65–8

After three months, Huck has learned to read and write. Finding his father's boot-tracks in the snow (p. 66), he tries to prevent Pap's re-entry into his life by selling his fortune to Judge Thatcher for one dollar (p. 67). Huck asks Jim to consult his hair-ball to find out what is going to happen (p. 67). When he goes up to bed that night, he finds Pap in his room.

CHAPTER 5, pp. 69–73

Pap is sarcastic about Huck's changed way of life. He has come to seize Huck's money and finds a new judge who rules that he can reclaim Huck from Mrs Douglas and Judge Thatcher (pp. 71–2). Pap keeps on getting drunk. The new judge takes him into his house and Pap signs the pledge – but soon relapses.

CHAPTER 6, pp. 74–81

In his efforts to get control of Huck and his money, Pap becomes a nuisance to everyone. He kidnaps Huck (p. 74) and takes him to a log cabin, locking him in whenever he goes away. Huck quite enjoys himself, except for Pap's beatings and his long periods of solitude. He plans to escape (p. 75). One night Pap has an attack of delirium tremens in which he tries to kill Huck (p. 80). Only Pap's exhaustion saves the boy.

CHAPTER 7, pp. 82–8

The June floods bring down a canoe (p. 82), which Huck hides in the undergrowth of the river bank. While Pap is away, Huck fakes his own murder (p. 85) and makes his getaway just as Pap returns (p. 87). Huck paddles downstream and hides on Jackson's Island.

CHAPTER 8, pp. 89–100

The next day, Huck watches a steamboat search for his corpse (pp. 90–91). After three days of camping out on the island, he finds a fire still smoking (p. 92). He hides in alarm and then crosses to the Illinois shore, but is driven back by the sound of voices. He spends a sleepless night. At daybreak, he comes across Jim (p. 74). The slave explains he has run away because Miss Watson was going to sell him 'down the river'. They have a long and friendly conversation.

CHAPTER 9, pp. 101–5

Jim and Huck find a cave at the top of a ridge and Jim suggests they should move their stores in because it is going to rain (p. 101). After a violent storm, the river rises for twelve days. It brings down part of a log raft and a frame house (p. 103), from which they take several items. There is a dead man in the house; Jim stops Huck from looking at his face.

CHAPTER 10, pp. 106–9

Huck plays a trick on Jim with a dead rattlesnake. The animal's mate enters the cave and bites Jim (p. 107). Jim is seriously ill for four days. Huck becomes bored (p. 109) and returns to the outskirts of St

Petersburg, disguised as a girl. He sees a light burning in a house long unoccupied. When he sees an unknown woman inside, he decides to enter.

CHAPTER 11, pp. 110–17

The woman is Judith Loftus, a newcomer to the town, from whom Huck learns the town's reaction to his 'death'. Both Pap and Jim are being blamed for the 'murder'. Mrs Loftus reveals (p. 112) that she has seen smoke on Jackson's Island. Her husband and a friend are about to set out there to hunt for the runaway slave. Huck gives himself away to Mrs Loftus, who has already guessed that he is a boy (p. 112). He spins a more plausible story and she sends him away with a warning to be more careful. Huck rushes back to warn Jim (p. 117) and they set off on the raft.

CHAPTER 12, pp. 118–25

They drift down the Mississippi for five days, hiding by day and travelling by night. During a storm they come across a wrecked steamboat (p. 121) and Huck persuades Jim to come aboard with him. They find a party of cutthroats in the officers' cabin; in alarm, they try to leave but find that the raft has broken loose.

CHAPTER 13, pp. 126–31

They manage to escape in the cutthroats' boat. They overtake their raft (p. 128) and Huck sends Jim ahead while he tries to persuade the watchman on a ferry-boat to rescue the robbers from the steamboat. The attempt is too late. Huck catches up with Jim a little before dawn.

CHAPTER 14, pp. 132–6

The plunder from the robbers' boat leads to an amusing conversation between Huck and Jim about 'kings, and dukes, and earls, and such' (p. 132) and 'ole King Sollermun'. There is an argument and Huck fails to bring Jim round to his point of view.

CHAPTER 15, pp. 137–43

The raft is approaching Cairo, at the junction of the Mississippi and the Ohio, from where they can take a steamboat to the free states. The raft is torn from its mooring (p. 137) and the two friends become separated, as Huck is in the canoe. When he catches up with the raft, he pretends that the whole episode was a dream (p. 140). Jim is deeply hurt when he realizes that Huck has made a fool of him (p. 143); he rebukes Huck with great dignity. Huck is ashamed and forces himself to apologize to Jim.

CHAPTER 16, pp. 144–53

Huck's 'conscience' overwhelms him; he makes up his mind to hand Jim over (p. 146), but when approached by two slave hunters finds he cannot do it (p. 147) and makes up another elaborate story to save his friend. They have overshot Cairo in the fog (p. 150) but are prevented from paddling back by the loss of the canoe (p. 151). That night the raft is run down by a steamboat (p. 152). Huck struggles ashore and walks until he comes to a large house, where he is surrounded by a pack of dogs (p. 153).

CHAPTER 17, pp. 154–63

Huck assumes yet another identity and is taken in by the Grangerfords, a wealthy local family. He becomes friendly with the youngest son, Buck. He describes the house and is particularly struck by the memorials of Emmeline Grangerford, who died at the age of fifteen.

CHAPTER 18, pp. 164–76

The other members of the family are described. Huck finds out about the feud with the Shepherdsons (p. 167). After church on Sunday, Huck runs back to fetch Miss Sophia's Testament (p. 169) and discovers a message inside, which he pretends he cannot read (p. 171). One of the slaves leads Huck to the swamp; Jim is hiding there and being looked after by the Grangerfords' slaves. The next day Huck learns that the 'message' has led to Sophia eloping with Harney Shepherdson. There is a shoot-up between the two families. Huck is a horrified spectator of the slaughter (p. 174) and sees his friend Buck killed (p. 175). He runs away to find Jim and they set out on the raft.

CHAPTER 19, pp. 177–86

Life becomes peaceful again until Huck rescues two tricksters being pursued by men and dogs (p. 180). They join the raft, claiming to be respectively the rightful Duke of Bridgewater and the 'pore disappeared Dauphin' of France. Huck sees through them but says nothing to Jim, for the sake of preserving harmony on the raft.

CHAPTER 20, pp. 187–96

Huck pretends that Jim is his own slave to lull the conmen's suspicions (p. 187). He accompanies the king to a revival meeting, where the old rogue takes a handsome collection (p. 194) by pretending to be a reformed pirate. Meantime, the duke has been printing off a handbill which will allow them to travel safely during the daytime.

CHAPTER 21, pp. 197–207

The duke and the king rehearse some scenes from Shakespeare and land at a small town in Arkansaw (p. 199). Huck goes with them to put up the posters advertising their performance (p. 200). He describes the loafers of the town (pp. 201–2) and an incident in which a boastful drunk named Boggs is shot down by a Colonel Sherburn (p. 205).

CHAPTER 22, pp. 208–13

The townspeople mob Sherburn's house, intending to lynch him; but when he makes a contemptuous speech (pp. 209–10) and cocks his gun, they run away. Huck visits a touring circus and is delighted by the skill of the riders (pp. 210–11). He earnestly describes the antics of a 'drunken' clown. The Shakespearian performance is a dismal failure (p. 213), so the duke switches to low comedy – the Royal Nonesuch (p. 213).

CHAPTER 23, pp. 214–19

The audience are furious at being 'had' by the duke and king, but keep quiet about it in the town for fear of ridicule (p. 215). After taking the ticket money on the third night the king and duke make a bolt for it (p. 216). Jim is shocked by their behaviour and Huck gives him a garbled history lesson (p. 217), proving that 'all kings is mostly rapscallions'. The next morning, Jim recalls with deep remorse an incident in which he struck his little daughter (p. 219).

CHAPTER 24, pp. 220–26

Jim complains about being tied up all day, so the duke disguises him as a 'Sick Arab', with a notice that will deter inquisitive snoopers and

Synopsis of Huckleberry Finn: **Chapter 25, pp. 227–34** 13

leaves him free (p. 220). Casting around for a 'project', the king extracts details of the Wilks family. The three nieces of Peter Wilks, lately deceased, are awaiting the arrival of two more uncles (one a deaf-mute) from England, with whom they will divide the inheritance. The king begins to organize the fraud, taking the speaking part for himself. Huck is amazed when the townspeople accept the two impostors as Harvey and William Wilks.

CHAPTER 25, pp. 227–34

The king and duke put on a display of grief beside their 'brother's' coffin (p. 228) and receive a letter which leads them to a hoard of six thousand dollars in gold. They make up a slight deficit out of their own pockets and present the whole sum to the girls (p. 231). This 'boss dodge' so impresses the neighbours that they turn against a Dr Robinson, who tries to denounce the two frauds (p. 233). To show her confidence in him, the eldest girl, Mary Jane, asks the king to invest the money for herself and her sisters (p. 234).

CHAPTER 26, pp. 235–43

When Joanna, the youngest girl, expresses doubts about Huck's claims to be an English valet, her sisters make her apologize (p. 239). Huck is ashamed at the way he is standing by while the king and duke cheat the girls out of their inheritance. He finds out where the king has hidden the money and removes it to his own room.

CHAPTER 27, pp. 244–51

Huck is interrupted when he takes the gold downstairs, meaning to hide it somewhere out of doors. He is forced to conceal it in the coffin

(p. 244). There is no chance to retrieve it before the funeral service and burial (p. 247). After selling off the slaves (p. 248), the king and duke find out that the gold has disappeared; Huck manages to convince them that the slaves have taken it with them (p. 249).

CHAPTER 28, pp. 252–62

Huck tells Mary Jane that her 'uncles' are frauds (p. 252); he persuades her to leave town for a few days to avoid them, giving her a note to say where the gold is hidden. He spins a story to account for her absence to her sisters (pp. 258–9). During the auction of Peter Wilks's property, the real brothers arrive.

CHAPTER 29, pp. 263–73

Dr Robinson and the lawyer arrange a series of tests to settle which set of brothers is genuine. The king manages to wriggle out of each awkward situation and the neighbours finally agree to decide the question by digging up the body. As they discover the bag of gold, Huck makes his escape and rejoins Jim on the raft (p. 272). Their relief is short-lived for the king and duke soon catch them up (p. 273).

CHAPTER 30, pp. 274–7

Huck pretends that he ran out on the king and duke because he was afraid of being hanged (p. 274), and the two charlatans begin to quarrel, each suspecting the other of trying to cheat him. The king, in danger of being choked, confesses his 'guilt'. As they sleep off their drunken reconciliation, Huck tells Jim the real story.

CHAPTER 31, pp. 278–87

The conmen have a run of bad luck. After going into town on a mysterious errand, the king is found drunk in a 'doggery' (p. 279). Huck runs back to the raft but Jim has disappeared. He learns from a local boy (p. 280) that Jim has been sold for reward money to the owner of Phelps's farm. After a struggle with his conscience, Huck sets out to rescue Jim and runs into the duke (p. 284). The duke tries to send him inland to look for Jim and Huck pretends to believe him (p. 286).

CHAPTER 32, pp. 288–94

At the farm, Mrs Phelps greets Huck as if she is expecting him (p. 290) and tells him to call her 'Aunt Sally'. When 'Uncle Silas' also appears (p. 292), Huck finds that he is being mistaken for Tom Sawyer – a part he can of course play to perfection. On the pretext of going to collect his luggage, he sets out for town to intercept the real Tom and explain the situation.

CHAPTER 33, pp. 295–302

When the boys meet, Huck confesses that he intends to steal Jim (p. 296). Huck is astonished that the respectable Tom Sawyer wants to join in. Huck returns to the farm and Tom turns up later. He amuses himself by pretending to be a stranger and then passes himself off as his own brother, Sid. Jim has told Mr Phelps about the Royal Nonesuch and the townspeople are going to drive the king and duke out of town (p. 301). Huck goes with Tom to warn them but arrives too late: they have already been tarred and feathered.

CHAPTER 34, pp. 303–9

Tom and Huck find out where Jim is locked up but Tom considers Huck's plan of escape too simple (p. 304). They trick Nat, Jim's keeper, into allowing them to enter the cabin with him and persuade him that their conversation with Jim is a delusion caused by 'witches'.

CHAPTER 35, pp. 310–17

Tom devises various methods of making Jim's escape as complicated as possible, following the best traditions of romantic fiction. They will dig him out of the hut – but with case-knives.

CHAPTER 36, pp. 318–23

The digging makes the boys' hands so sore that they have to revert to using a pick-axe, but Tom insists on calling it a case-knife. On the second night, they break through. Like Huck, Jim thinks very little of Tom's plans, but agrees to them because they are 'white folks and knowed better than him' (p. 321). Various articles are smuggled in; Nat, the Negro slave who feeds Jim, thinks the witches are after him again when the farm dogs get in through the hole dug by Tom and Huck (p. 322). Tom promises to bake a pie to appease the 'witches'.

CHAPTER 37, pp. 324–30

Aunt Sally is perplexed by the disappearance of household articles taken by the boys for Jim. They further confuse her by making some of them mysteriously reappear and then vanish again (p. 328). A sheet is removed from the washing line and sent into Jim's cabin as a rope-ladder, baked inside a 'witch-pie'.

CHAPTER 38, pp. 331–7

Tom says that Jim must scratch his coat of arms and an inscription on his prison wall before escaping, because 'all the nobility does' (p. 332). As a log surface is unsuitable, they make Jim come to the mill with them to help them roll back a huge grindstone (pp. 333–4). Tom wants Jim to keep a pet – a snake, spider or rat – and raise a flower by watering it with his tears.

CHAPTER 39, pp. 338–43

The boys fill Jim's cabin with 'pets', although some escape round the house while awaiting delivery (p. 339). After three weeks, Tom decides it is time to send out the 'nonnamous' letters giving warning of Jim's intended escape (p. 340). These cause great alarm to the Phelpses (p. 342).

CHAPTER 40, pp. 344–50

At the time proposed for the escape, Huck discovers that fifteen men with guns are about to surround Jim's hut. He rushes off to warn Tom, who is already at the hut (p. 346). They escape with Jim, bullets whistling round them, as the farmers pound after them in hot pursuit. In the darkness, the three fugitives escape and cross to Spaniard's Island, where Huck's raft is hidden (p. 348). There Tom tells the others that he has a bullet in the calf of his leg. Despite his protests, Jim and Huck refuse to set out. Huck goes to town to look for a doctor.

CHAPTER 41, pp. 351–8

The doctor from Pikesville insists on crossing to the island on his own and Huck spends the night in a lumber pile. Next morning, he runs

18 *Passnotes:* **The Adventures of Huckleberry Finn**

into Uncle Silas, who takes Huck home, expecting 'Sid' to follow (p. 353). The house is full of neighbours, discussing Jim's escape. Aunt Sally's anxiety when 'Sid' has still not turned up by nightfall makes Huck feel very guilty. He keeps his promise not to go out of the house that night.

CHAPTER 42, pp. 359–67

Mr Phelps hands his wife a letter he had collected from the post-office the day before (p. 359). Before she can read it, the doctor returns with Tom, carried on a mattress, delirious. Jim is with them, tied and bound. The doctor stops the farmers from lynching Jim by telling them how he had helped him look after Tom. The doctor had remained on Spaniard's Island until he could summon help to seize Jim (p. 361). Jim is locked up again (p. 362). When Tom recovers from his fever, he talks gleefully about his 'evasion' scheme. When he hears that Jim has not escaped, he reveals that Jim had been freed two months before, in Miss Watson's will (p. 365). Aunt Polly (Tom's guardian) unexpectedly enters: she has become suspicious at the mention of 'Sid' in her sister's letters and has received no answer to her inquiries. (Tom, of course, has hidden them.).

CHAPTER 43, pp. 368–9 (CHAPTER THE LAST)

Tom tells Huck that he had intended to sail down to the mouth of the Mississippi and then bring Jim back home in style on a steamboat (p. 368). Jim is quickly released. Tom wants them all to go to the Territory 'for howling adventures amongst the Injuns' (p. 369); he tells Huck his six thousand dollars are still safe – Pap has never come back. Jim reveals that the dead man in the frame house (p. 103) was Pap. Finally, alarmed at the prospect of being 'sivilized' again, this time by Aunt Sally, Huck tells us he reckons that he's 'got to light out for the Territory ahead of the rest' (p. 369).

An Account of the Plot

CHAPTER 1, pp. 49–52

Huck begins his story by making a direct link with an earlier part of his life: 'You don't know about me, without you have read a book by the name of *The Adventures of Tom Sawyer*' (p. 49). He reminds us that he and Tom had found a treasure of 'six thousand dollars apiece – all gold' and that he had been adopted by the Widow Douglas, who intended to 'sivilize' him. After three weeks, Huck had escaped back to his old way of life but was persuaded to give civilized life another try by the promise of being allowed to join Tom's band of robbers. 'So I went back,' says Huck and begins his story. We hear about the widow's efforts to reform him by putting him into uncomfortable clothing, by regular and formal meals, a ban on smoking and bible instruction. Because Huck doesn't 'take no stock in no dead people' (p. 50), he finds the last quite mystifying. The widow's sister, Miss Watson, 'a tolerable slim old maid, with goggles on' (p. 50), also takes a hand in trying to educate Huck, with no more success. After family prayers Huck goes to sit at his bedroom window, staring out at the night. He is restless and miserable. 'I felt so lonesome I most wished I was dead' (p. 51). He is frightened by the noises he hears outside the house – birds and other animals, and a 'ghost' – but they obviously make more sense to him than the beliefs and behaviour that the two women are trying to force on him. The sounds outside are interpreted by Huck as omens of death. 'Down-hearted and scared', he wishes for company and immediately a spider falls into his candle – an even worse sign. He carries out all the actions recommended for turning bad luck into good but they do not cheer him up. He is 'shaking all over' (p. 52) and takes out his pipe for a smoke. Just after a town clock strikes midnight he hears Tom Sawyer's signal among the trees. Huck scrambles out of the window to join his friend.

This first chapter takes us instantly into the conflict that will start Huck off on his search for freedom. The well-meant efforts of the two women to impose conventional behaviour on the ragamuffin Huck are doomed to failure. They are also very funny. The rest of the chapter operates on a deeper level and the style changes. Huck's instant response to experience and his openness to primitive superstitions come over as an overheard monologue, rather than as straightforward description, even though both sections are directly addressed to the reader. Linking the two is the theme of death, treated first in an amusing or farcical way – 'the bad place' and 'the good place' (pp. 50 and 51) and then with much darker overtones. You will find other examples of this double treatment thoughout the novel. Look out for them: they are important when we come to discuss the final chapters. (See 'The Ending of *The Adventures of Huckleberry Finn*', p. 91.).

CHAPTER 2, pp. 53–9

As Huck and Tom make their way out of the garden, Huck trips over a root. The noise is heard by Jim, Miss Watson's Negro slave, who comes to investigate. For some minutes the three of them are within touching distance but Jim cannot see the boys. Huck and Tom do not dare to move. Then Jim falls asleep and they creep away. Tom says he needs some candles and they return to take these from the kitchen. After Tom has played a trick on the sleeping Jim, he takes Huck to a tanyard where several other members of the gang are waiting for them. They untie a skiff and go down river for two and a half miles to a cave in the hillside. The rest of the chapter is taken up with the boys' conversation as Tom explains the rules of his robber-band. These are taken from romantic novels of adventure. Tom's blood-thirsty plans are made to seem ridiculous by his ignorance of the terms he is using. When one of the gang asks the meaning of 'ransomed', Tom replies, 'I don't know. But that's what they do. I've seen it in books; and so of course that's what we've got to do' (p. 57). Huck's isolation is once more underlined: he has no family to offer for execution, if he betrays the gang. He is 'most ready to cry' (p. 57), until he thinks of offering Miss Watson as a victim. On these terms, he is allowed to join. The gang decide to 'meet next week and rob somebody and kill some people' (p. 59). After that, they end their meeting and all go home. Huck crawls in through his window with his clothes 'all greased up and clayey' (p. 59).

Notice here how Huck's isolation from St Petersburg society influences even his status among other boys. Some points are sketched out here that will be important later in the book: riding down the Mississippi; the closeness of Huck and Jim — at this stage a near-contact with no meaning; and we are reminded of Pap, Huck's drunken father, who is to make a terrifying re-entry into his son's life.

CHAPTER 3, pp. 60–64

Miss Watson tries to redeem Huck through prayer; but Huck's hard life has pared down the way he looks at the world to a devastating simplicity: when Mrs Douglas tries to explain that he must pray for 'spiritual gifts' Huck decides that her kind of prayer will only benefit other people, not himself (p. 60). A body is found in the river; Huck is told that this is his father, but 'knows' that as the corpse was found floating on its back — not its face — it must be that of a woman dressed in man's clothes. He is becoming disillusioned with the exploits of Tom's gang. The promised thrills turn out to be very tame: they jump out from behind trees on people going to market and 'bust up' a Sunday-school picnic — but even then they are chased away from their loot by the teacher in charge. This is supposed to be a raid on 'a whole parcel of Spanish merchants and rich A–rabs' (p. 62). The literal-minded Huck complains that he did not see any of the promised 'di'monds'. Tom puts this down to the evil work of magicians and genies, who have changed the appearance of things 'out of spite'. He quotes *Don Quixote* as proof, unaware that Cervantes' tale was written to ridicule just such extravagant fantasies. Huck tries to summon up a genie by rubbing a lamp; he concludes in disgust 'all that stuff was only just one of Tom Sawyer's lies . . . It had all the marks of a Sunday school' (p. 64). These words pointedly link Miss Watson's religious beliefs with tales of unlikely adventures. Twain implies that both are false and makes Huck reject both.

CHAPTER 4, pp. 65–8

Three or four months pass by, during which Huck becomes half-reconciled to forming part of a small-town society. However, he finds it hard to bear the nagging of Miss Watson, who is much less gentle with him than her sister. One day, after a new fall of snow, Huck sees the distinctive boot-tracks of his father and fears that Pap has returned, intending to get hold of his money. His immediate reaction is to rush to Judge Thatcher (another character from *The Adventures of Tom Sawyer*) and try to hand it over to him. Shaking off his father is far more important to Huck than keeping his fortune. The judge 'buys' the money from Huck for one dollar (p. 67), although we learn at the end of the book that he keeps it safe for him. Huck then goes to Jim and asks him to tell his fortune by using an old hair-ball from an ox's stomach. Jim tells him. 'You wants to keep 'way fum de water as much as you kin' (p. 68) – the exact opposite of what follows. When Huck goes upstairs that night he finds Pap sitting in his room.

The final sentence of the chapter takes us abruptly from imaginary adventures into brutal reality. Pap's re-entry has been led up to by the mention of him in two previous chapters. From now on Huck will witness – and sometimes be involved in – real violence and murder.

CHAPTER 5, pp. 69–73

Huck's involvement with his father begins on an almost humorous note, despite the sinister description of the broken-down old drunk: 'There warn't no color in his face ... it was white ... a tree-toad white, a fish-belly white' (p. 69). Pap scolds his son for putting on 'considerble many frills' and, as Huck had feared, has returned for Huck's money. He pours scorn on what he sees as Huck's attempts to 'let on to be better'n what *he* is' (p. 70). This kind of outburst is repeated in the next chapter, when Pap makes a savagely racist attack on an educated Negro. Pap takes Huck's one dollar and goes out to get drunk. Next day he tries to lay his hands on the six thousand dollars. The widow and Judge Thatcher go to law to gain custody of

Huck but a new judge overrules them. After Pap has been on a 'bender', this second judge takes him in and tries to reform him. The crafty old man exploits his hosts, promising that he is 'agoing to turn over a new leaf' (p. 72) in a scene that satirizes do-gooders and false piety. Pap relapses into bad habits and the judge's reaction shows us how limited is the charity of these so-called Christian townsfolk.

This chapter forms a bridge between the children's games of Tom Sawyer's gang and the violent scenes that follow. Note Huck's totally realistic view of his father. He does not like him but he does not judge him either – merely tries to avoid him. This is a good moment to start comparing father and son: one of the points you will have to consider is whether Twain intends us to see Pap as an older version of Huck. Will Huck become like his father, once he had lost the innocence of childhood and meets the hard realities of trying to live as a free-wheeling outsider?

CHAPTER 6, pp. 74–81

Pap continues to hang around the town, pestering Huck for money, and tries to sue Judge Thatcher for the whole fortune. When the widow threatens him, in revenge Pap kidnaps Huck and takes him three miles up river to a log cabin on the Illinois side. (See map on p. 11.) Pap locks the door at night and whenever he goes to the store for groceries and whisky. 'I never got a chance to run off,' says Huck (p. 74). However, it is obvious that he is enjoying a return to his old kind of life and could have run off if he had really tried. 'It was kind of lazy and jolly, laying off comfortable all day, smoking and fishing, and no books nor study ... I didn't want to go back no more' (p. 75). But there are two drawbacks: whenever Pap is drunk, he beats Huck and, during his long absences, Huck feels 'lonesome'. He begins to prepare for escape by sawing away one of the bottom logs of the hut. He is interrupted by Pap's return from town. Pap has heard that there is to be another trial about who is to be Huck's guardian – himself or the widow – and it is thought that this time Mrs Douglas will win the case. 'He said ... if they tried to come any such game on him he knowed of a place six or seven mile off, to stow me in' (p. 76). Huck is alarmed by both possibilities: he doesn't want to go back to Widow Douglas but he does not like the thought of being taken away by Pap, either. He decides that he will escape that night 'if Pap got drunk enough' (p. 77). While Huck cooks their supper, Pap denounces the 'govment' for allowing a man's son to be taken away from him. He goes on to release all the prejudice and resentment of a 'poor white' against an educated Negro from Ohio, whom he had seen on election day. This man is not only well-dressed and well-off but he actually has the right to vote in his own state. 'I'll never vote agin,' says Pap (p. 78), outraged at this final insult to his status. Pap's outburst springs from envy, as well as the normal Southern acceptance of slavery. 'I says to the people, why ain't this nigger put up at auction and sold? . . . they said he couldn't be sold till he'd been in the State six months, and he hadn't been there that long yet' (p. 78). Up to this point Pap has been a comic, drunken figure, stumbling over objects in the cabin and cursing as he inflicts minor injuries on himself. He begins to drink more heavily; and Huck thinks he will be able to escape when his father falls into a drunken sleep. He has to wait for so long that he falls asleep himself and is roused by a terrified scream. He sees Pap 'looking wild and skipping around . . . and yelling about snakes' (p. 79). The old man is in the grip of delirium tremens, hallucinating and running round the cabin until he drops from exhaustion, moaning and crying. The scene is no longer amusing: in his agonized suffering Pap mistakes Huck for the Angel of Death and threatens to kill him with his clasp-knife. Only another fit of exhaustion saves Huck from his danger. When Pap finally passes out, Huck sits over him with a loaded rifle, waiting for the next outburst. Once more we see Twain's double approach to the same situation – farce has changed into terror.

CHAPTER 7, pp. 82–8

Huck falls asleep, holding the gun. Pap remembers nothing about his fit when he wakes up and Huck pretends that he is on guard because someone tried to get into the cabin during the night. Pap sends him out to check the fishing lines and Huck sees the river is flooding in the

'June rise'. Driftwood and pieces of log rafts are floating down. Huck swims out to catch a canoe, which he hides in a nearby creek under vines and willows. Pap threatens to shoot the next intruder and this gives Huck an idea for his escape. He goes out in the skiff with Pap to tow in part of a log raft, which Pap wants to sell to a timber-yard in town. While he is away, Huck finishes sawing his way out of the cabin and removes everything useful to stow in his canoe. He goes into the woods and shoots a wild pig. When he returns, he hacks in the cabin door with the wood-axe, smears the pig's blood over this and the earth floor of the cabin, and tears out some of his own hair to put on the axe. Then he lays two false trails – one to make it look as if the 'murderer' has gone inland and another to make Pap think that his body has been dumped in the river. Huck lies low in the canoe until night-time. He falls asleep. When he wakes up there is bright moonshine. 'Everything was dead quiet, and it looked late, and *smelt* late' (p. 86). He hears Pap rowing towards him, so he strikes out into the middle of the river and lies down in the canoe until he has drifted down to Jackson's Island, where he lands, hides the canoe and takes a nap before breakfast.

Huck's practical intelligence supplies him with a gruesome but effective plan of escape. Twain makes sure that we compare it with the make-believe of Tom Sawyer by having Huck wish for Tom's 'fancy touches' (p. 85). Huck's pretended 'death' has perhaps a deeper symbolic meaning (see 'Themes', p. 81 and 'Imagery and Symbolism, p. 79). A sense of relief floods the narrative, as Huck wriggles out of the stifling confinement of the cabin and reaches the banks of the river to set out on his adventure. His isolation is stressed by the voices that come across the water and the distant lights of the town (p. 87), and above all by the enormous width of the river, 'miles and miles across' (p. 86). Huck's dominant feeling is a sense of relief and tranquillity; he is no longer 'lonesome'.

CHAPTER 8, pp. 89–100

Huck wakes up feeling 'powerful lazy and comfortable' (p. 89) and sees a steamboat looking for his 'remainders'. The firing of cannon is supposed to bring his body to the surface, as is the bread that floats down, injected with quicksilver (mercury). Huck seizes one of the loaves, reflecting that there must be something in prayer after all, since the bread was meant to find him. Everyone he knows in St Petersburg is on board the steamboat, which passes close by him as he hides on the island. For three days Huck is absolutely free to live the way he wants and is 'feeling pretty satisfied' (p. 91) – then the word 'lonesome' creeps in again. The next day Huck comes across traces of a recent camp fire. In fright, he hides until it is dark and he can paddle over to the Illinois shore. Hearing voices in the woods there, he returns to the island and, after a disturbed night, decides that he must find out who is sharing the island with him. At daybreak, he finds Miss Watson's slave, Jim, sleeping beside a fire. Jim is terrified because he thinks that Huck is a ghost. They have breakfast together and Jim confesses that he has run away. Miss Watson had promised Jim that she would never sell him down to New Orleans. A slave trader had appeared in the district and Jim had heard Miss Watson tell her sister that she couldn't resist the offer of eight hundred dollars for him. Jim had immediately run away and hid all night. Knowing that the dogs would track him if he escaped on foot, and that a stolen boat would be missed, he had waited for a raft to come drifting down. He had planned to go downstream about twenty-five miles and then swim ashore to the free state of Illinois. He had to leave the raft when a man had come towards him with a lantern. (The 'raft' here is one of the huge constructions of logs used to float timber down the Mississippi and which carried a crew of about half a dozen men.) Huck has already promised not to betray Jim – even if people call him 'a low down Ab'litionist' (p. 96) – and they settle down for a long talk about signs of good and bad luck and Jim's unsuccessful attempts to become rich. He says, '. . . I'se rich now, come to look at it. I owns myself, en I's wuth eight hund'd dollars' (p. 100).

The Negro's superstitions are contrasted with the equally irrational beliefs of white people: cannon fire or floating bread will discover a dead body. The main theme of the chapter is the beginning of the friendship between Huck and Jim. Huck's promise not to 'tell' is given unthinkingly, out of good nature, and because he is glad of Jim's company. 'I was ever so glad to see Jim. I warn't lonesome, now' (p. 94). Even at this stage, however, Huck knows that he runs the risk of being thought an 'Abolitionist' – one of the people who crusaded actively for an end to slavery and whom Southerners regarded with horror. The struggle between Huck's 'sound heart' and his 'deformed conscience' has already inserted itself into the story.

CHAPTER 9, pp. 101–5

Huck knows Jackson's Island well from a previous expedition there with Tom Sawyer. Huck and Jim explore and find a cave. Jim's bird signs tell him that it is going to rain and he persuades Huck to move all the equipment from the canoe into the cave. There is a violent thunderstorm, followed by ten or twelve days of rising floods which cover the lower parts of the island. They catch a small section of a lumber raft: 'twelve foot wide and about fifteen or sixteen foot long, and the top stood above water six or seven inches' (p. 103). The floods also bring down a two-storey frame house; they paddle over to it and tie alongside, but have to wait for daylight before they can go over its contents. Inside, they find many useful objects – also the body of a dead man, shot in the back. Jim stops Huck from looking at the face – 'it's too gashly' (p. 103). The full extent of his care for Huck in doing this is not revealed until the last chapter. Huck in turn makes Jim lie down in the canoe, out of sight, in case he is spotted from the shore – a mark of his growing affection for Jim.

Notice the superb description of the storm – a fine example of the effects Twain could achieve through Huck's narrative voice. The dialect gives the impression of an ungrammatical piling up of detail, as Huck responds directly to his experience of the storm, but the apparent simplicity of style conceals great artistic skill.

CHAPTER 10, pp. 106–9

Jim tries to stop Huck talking about the dead man by saying it will bring them bad luck. Huck argues against this superstitious behaviour and mocks the way Jim had warned him about handling a snakeskin two days before: have they not obtained a lot of useful articles from the house and eight silver dollars as well? The bad luck does come, when Huck puts a rattlesnake he had killed on Jim's blanket for a joke, and at night the snake's mate enters the cave and bites Jim on the heel. Jim is laid up for four days, delirious part of the time; and Huck follows his instructions for a cure – roast rattlesnake and whisky. The river goes down and they catch an enormous cat-fish. The thought of how much they could have sold it for makes Huck realize that life on the island is getting 'slow and dull' (p. 108). He wants to 'slip over the river' to find out what is going on. Jim warns him to be careful and suggests that Huck should dress up in some of the clothes taken from the house. He helps Huck to disguise himself as a girl and Huck paddles the canoe to the outskirts of St Petersburg. He sees an unknown woman knitting inside a shanty house unoccupied for a long time and knocks at the door.

This is the first of many false identities that Huck will take on during his trip down the river. The snake episode shows that the connection between superstition and truth is not a simple one: Huck, too, has his own superstitions; and some taboos – for example, not meddling with snakes, dead or alive – may be based on sound common sense.

CHAPTER 11, pp. 110–17

Judith Loftus, the woman Huck has seen through the window, is the first of many characters in the novel who appear for one episode only. Huck spins a plausible story and at first Mrs Loftus accepts it. After chatting about herself and her family, she repeats what people in the town are saying about Huck's 'murder' (pp. 111-12). Suspicion has fastened on Pap Finn, who has gone off with two strangers, and on Jim. There is a reward of three hundred dollars for Jim's recapture. Mrs Loftus thinks Jim may be hiding on Jackson's Island – she has seen smoke rising from it (p. 112). Her husband and another man are going over to the island to investigate after midnight. Huck's alarm makes him seek distraction by threading a needle. Mrs Loftus notices how clumsy Huck is and once again asks his name. 'M – Mary

Williams,' says Huck (p. 113). 'I thought you said it was Sarah,' the woman replies. She tests Huck's throwing abilities, and the way he catches a piece of lead, and her suspicions grow. She says she knows he is a boy, not a girl, but thinks he is a runaway apprentice. She says she will not give him away if only he will tell her the truth. Huck seizes eagerly on this idea and pretends to have escaped from a mean old farmer thirty miles away. After testing him on three 'country' questions, Mrs Loftus gives Huck some food for his journey and promises to help if he gets into trouble again. He hurries back to the island and starts a fire to deceive the search party, and then rushes into the cave to arouse Jim. 'Git up and hump yourself, Jim! There ain't a minute to lose. They're after us!' (p. 117). They load up the raft and begin to sail down river, with the canoe tied beside them.

The most significant point in this episode is the use of the word 'us'. Huck is officially dead, so no one is pursuing him; but he has now committed himself to his friendship with Jim, and their separate quests for freedom have become one. As they journey on, this link between them will be put to severe tests.

CHAPTER 12, pp. 118–25

The raft drifts down the Mississippi until dawn, when they moor it, and stay in hiding. Jim thinks Mrs Loftus is 'a smart one' and will have told her husband to get a dog to track them – and his delay in doing this is the only reason why their slow-moving raft has not been overtaken. Jim builds a shelter on the raft and fits it with a hearth. He also raises the floor so that they will not be washed over by waves from passing steamboats. They slip into a routine of travelling by night and tying up by day, taking fruit and vegetables and an occasional chicken from the fields, and buying other food from the little village stores. On the fifth night, below St Louis, they almost run into a wrecked steamboat lying on its side. Huck wants to go aboard but Jim is 'dead against it'. In the end he lets himself be overruled as Huck is so anxious to give the boat a 'rummaging' (p. 122). The boat is in darkness but as they explore they see a light in the 'texas' – the officers' cabin. Huck crawls forward and sees two cutthroats who have tied up a third man and are planning to murder him. After an argument the men decide it will be better to leave their victim to drown when the steamboat breaks up. Huck wants to set the robbers' skiff adrift and then tell the Sheriff, so that all three will be caught. He goes back for Jim, who tells him that their raft has broken loose.

Notice the contrast of style in this chapter. The first section describes the relaxed, happy life led by Huck and Jim on their raft. The majesty of the river is conveyed in a poetic passage of great beauty: 'It was kind of solemn, drifting down the big still river, laying on our backs looking up at the stars . . . it warn't often that we laughed, only a little kind of a low chuckle' (p. 119). The adventure on the 'steamboat that had killed herself on a rock' begins abruptly and the chapter ends in breathless suspense. Huck's curiosity has led the two friends into an escapade that is potentially disastrous, as they blunder into a situation that is part of the violence and cruelty of river society. Later, we learn that the wrecked steamboat is named *Walter Scott*. Twain held Sir Walter Scott's novels responsible for the corruption of Southern society, which he saw as being riddled with violence under a veneer of false chivalry. The steamboat is here associated with thieves and murderers; the point is underlined by another reference to Tom Sawyer (p. 122).

CHAPTER 13, pp. 126–31

Huck and Jim know that their only hope of safety is to take the thieves' skiff for themselves. They crawl in darkness along the side of the overturned steamboat until they find it. Just as they are going to jump in, the two men come towards them carrying their loot. The thieves suddenly remember that their victim still has his share and return to take it from him. Huck cuts the boat's mooring ropes and Jim rows them downstream. Huck begins to worry about the robbers whom they have left to drown with their victim. 'I begun to think how dreadful it was, even for murderers, to be in such a fix. I says to myself, there ain't no telling but I might come to be a murderer myself, yet, and then how would *I* like it? . . . I'll . . . get somebody to go for that gang' – but he adds without seeing the contradiction, 'so they can be hung when their time comes' (p. 127). However, a storm prevents Huck and Jim from contacting anyone on shore and they drift downstream until the storm begins to die away and a flash of lightning shows the raft ahead of them. Huck sends Jim aboard the raft and rows towards a shore light. He comes across a ferry-boat and spins his most elaborate story yet. He tells the watchman that his family are aboard the doomed steamboat with the niece of Jim Hornback – a wealthy local man whom the watchman has already mentioned. Huck feels 'ruther comfortable on accounts of taking all this trouble for that gang' (p. 131), knowing that the widow would have approved of his action, and he pulls in to watch the ferry-boat start off on its rescue mission. Before this can happen, the wrecked steamboat slides by, 'dim and dusky' and low down in the water. Huck calls out but there is no answer. 'I felt a little bit heavy-hearted about the gang, but not much, for I reckoned if they could stand it, I could' (p. 131). Huck overtakes Jim on the raft and the two friends land on an island to sleep off the night's adventures.

Huck's sympathy for the robbers shows his instinctive kindness towards people in trouble. His feelings are genuine but not long-lived. He has a child's capacity to recover quickly from sorrow – an essential feature in allowing us to enjoy the humour of the book, which is heavily loaded with violence and brutality. As in the scene with Mrs Loftus (Chapter 11), we see Twain's genius for bestowing vivid, individualized dialogue even on minor characters who make only a brief appearance.

CHAPTER 14, pp. 132–6

This chapter is apparently only an amusing conversation between Huck and Jim, showing the progress of their friendship. The loot that the robbers had put into the skiff has now fallen to Huck and Jim. It includes clothes, books and cigars. Huck reads to Jim 'about kings, and dukes, and earls, and such, and how gaudy they dressed, and how much style they put on' (p. 132). Jim's naive questions lead to a discussion of Solomon's famous judgement about the child claimed by two women. Huck says that Jim has totally misunderstood the point of the story. He returns to the subject of royalty and comes unstuck on Jim's inability to grasp the concept of a foreign language, while Jim cleverly uses Huck's own form of reasoning against him. Huck concludes, '... you can't learn a nigger to argue. So I quit' (p. 136). His assumption of white superiority is to be roughly jolted in the next chapter.

This conversation is more significant than it appears. (Compare it with another, pp. 216–18, Chapter 23.) It anticipates the long series of incidents involving the sham king and duke who later invade the raft. Twain sees as much corruption and pretence in historical royal figures as in their modern counterparts: 'you couldn't tell them from the real kind' (p. 218). (See 'The king and the duke', pp. 72–3.).

CHAPTER 15, pp. 137–43

Jim's original plan had been to float far enough downstream to throw off pursuit and then swim to the free side of the river. He and Huck have now decided to go as far as Cairo, at the junction of the Ohio and the Mississippi, where they will sell the raft and travel by steamboat to the free states north of the Ohio. (See map on p. 11). They expect to take three more nights to reach Cairo. On the second night, a thick fog descends; Huck paddles ahead in the canoe, but the current is so strong that when he tries to tie up the raft it breaks from its mooring and he is separated from Jim. They cry out to each other in the fog but Huck is unable to make contact with the raft. 'I reckoned Jim had fetched up on a snag, maybe, and it was all up with him' (p. 139). Exhausted, he falls asleep and wakes up to clear starlight. He chases after two specks on the water and the second is their raft. Jim has dropped asleep over the steering oar. The raft is covered with leaves and other litter it has picked up on its course downstream. Huck plays a cruel trick when he gets aboard. He wakes Jim, who is overjoyed that Huck is safely back. Huck convinces Jim that the whole fog episode is something he imagined in a dream, calling him a 'tangle-headed old fool' (p. 141): he (Huck) has been on the raft all the time. He compounds his cruelty by urging Jim to interpret the 'dream', and allows him to do this. At the end Huck asks, 'but what does *these* things stand for' – the 'leaves and rubbish on the raft, and the smashed oar' (p. 142). Jim realizes that he is being mocked and is deeply hurt. He rebukes the boy in a simple and moving speech: 'Dat truck dah is *trash*; en trash is what people is dat puts dirt on de head er dey fren's en makes em ashamed' (p. 143). Huck feels 'mean' about his crude deception and goes to beg Jim's forgiveness, although 'It was fifteen minutes before I could work myself up to go and humble myself to a nigger' (p. 142).

This episode is one of the key moments in the book, when for the first time Huck becomes aware of Jim as a real human being. It is the first of three important occasions when Huck's true feelings wrench him out of his Southern-conditioned attitude towards slavery. (Ask yourself why Huck played his mean trick in the first place.)

CHAPTER 16, pp. 144–53

In this chapter Twain further opens up one of the main themes of the novel – the corruption that is inevitable in a slave-owning society and which affects even Huck Finn. It is demonstrated in the moral turmoil suffered by Huck, as his conscience battles with his heart. As they near Cairo – or think they do – Jim becomes more and more excited – 'all over trembly and feverish to be so close to freedom' (p. 145). Huck becomes more and more unhappy at the way he is helping Jim to escape. His language lapses into near-sentimentality: 'What did that poor old woman do to you, that you could treat her so mean? . . . she tried to be good to you every way she knowed how' (p. 145). Compare this with the crisp description of Miss Watson as 'a tolerable slim old maid, with goggles on' (p. 50). Jim is looking forward to paid work, so that he can buy his wife's freedom; 'then they would both work to buy the two children, and if their master wouldn't sell them, they'd get an Ab'litionist to go and steal them' (p. 146). Huck listens in horror; it is the last straw. He decides to paddle over to the first light he sees and give Jim up. When they seem to have reached Cairo, Jim helps Huck into the canoe, calling him 'de bes' fren' Jim's ever had' (p. 146). Their conversation is loaded with irony. 'Irony' is the opposite of what is really meant. Used deliberately by one character to another, it is almost the same as sarcasm. This is another type – someone assuming what is the opposite of the truth. The use of it here emphasizes the terrible dilemma Huck is in. Huck meets two men in a skiff, carrying guns. They are looking for escaped slaves. When he speaks to them he finds he isn't 'man enough – hadn't the spunk of a rabbit' (p. 147) to do what he intended. The men question him about passengers on the raft and Huck says the other man aboard is white. He asks for help to tow the raft ashore, and deceives the men into thinking that the man is his father and that he and the two women he says are aboard are all victims of smallpox. The slave-hunters back away hurriedly but float down forty dollars in gold to help Huck. They advise him to make sure of help next time before he mentions the 'smallpox' (p. 148). Huck returns to the raft, perplexed by his own behaviour after this second rejection of the social code. He decides that giving Jim up would have the same effect as not giving him up – he would 'feel bad'. In future he will 'always do whichever come handiest at the time' (p. 149). Back at the raft, Huck finds Jim hiding in the water with only his nose showing. He congratulates Huck on his 'dodge' and they divide the money between them. They drift past two more towns during the night; at daybreak they realize that they must have passed Cairo earlier in the fog and decide to abandon the raft and go back up the river by canoe. After sleeping out the day in a cottonwood thicket, they go back to their mooring at nightfall and find that the canoe has disappeared. There is nothing for it but to continue downstream on the raft until they have the chance to buy another canoe. Huck and Jim agree that their bad luck has been caused by the snake skin (Chapter 10). After three hours' drifting, a steamboat heads towards them 'looking like a black cloud with rows of glow-worms around it . . . her monstrous bows and guards hanging right over us' (p. 152). They light a lantern but it is too late – 'she come smashing straight through the raft' (p. 152). Huck dives to avoid the thirty-foot paddle-wheels and, when he surfaces, can see no signs of Jim. He manages to swim the two miles to the Kentucky shore, walks a little way and then finds himself outside a big house, being menaced by dogs.

This is the point at which Twain's first attempt to write the novel ended, in 1876, where the innocent comradeship of the raft is broken up by the steamboat, a dramatic symbol of the violence of life on and beside the river. It took him another seven years to finish the book (see Introduction), but the main themes had already been stated. The most important point is that Huck sees himself as doing wrong by helping Jim to escape – and particularly when he hears that Jim intends to steal his own children, which are someone else's 'property'. We must realize that it is only Huck's behaviour that changes, not his beliefs. These have been formed in a society whose values are based on a slave-owning economy. The corruption extends to all members of that society, however low their position in it.

CHAPTER 17, pp. 154–63

The barking of the dogs around Huck wakens the household. They are a family called Grangerford. Huck assumes another identity – George Jackson. Once assured that Huck does not belong to a rival family called Shepherdson, the Grangerfords take him in with true Southern hospitality. Huck invents another elaborate background for himself, but as usual cannot remember names accurately, and almost gives himself away to Buck, the youngest Grangerford, who is a boy of fourteen, like himself. Huck is very impressed with this old Southern family and their house, which he describes in great detail. Huck gives most attention to Emmeline Grangerford and her drawings and verses. This girl died at the age of fifteen; her room, unaltered and unused since her death, is kept as a kind of shrine to her memory. The description of all this is hilariously funny but, once more, Twain is using a double-edged approach. Emmeline is shown as being morbidly self-indulgent; she is obsessed with obituary notices. But the images of death and gloom, which are so absurd here, are about to be overtaken by a violent reality.

CHAPTER 18, pp. 164–76

Huck now describes the Grangerfords themselves. They are: mother, father, three sons and two daughters. They are handsome, charming and generous; their daily life exhibits a stately old-world courtesy. There had been three more sons but 'they got killed' (p. 165); we are not told how at this point. We learn that another family uses the same steamboat landing-place. Their name is Shepherdson and they are 'as high-toned, and well born, and rich and grand' (p. 166) as the Grangerfords. One day Huck is out hunting in the woods with Buck. A young man rides along the path and Buck makes them jump for cover. He takes a pot-shot which knocks the rider's hat off. Back home, Mr Grangerford rebukes Buck for not stepping openly into the road to shoot. When Huck asks for an explanation he is told 'it's on account of the feud' (p. 167) – a word that Huck does not understand. Buck says, 'A man has a quarrel with another ... and by-and-by everybody's killed off ... But it's kind of slow, and takes a long time' (p. 167). He does not know 'what the row was about in the first place', but recounts various incidents with great relish. He also praises the courage of the Shepherdsons: one of them managed to ride home wounded after beating off three Grangerfords – two of whom later died. Huck's questions draw out one horrifying detail after another. Huck describes a visit to the church which both families attend, carrying their guns. The sermon is about brotherly love: 'everybody said it was a good sermon, and they all talked it over going home' (p. 169). Twain rounds off the satire by making Huck become involved in a Romeo-and-Juliet-style romance between the two families, which ends not in reconciliation between them but in the extinction of the male Grangerfords. After dinner, Miss Sophia asks him to go back to the church and find her Testament, which she has left behind. Huck finds a mysterious message inside it. He pretends that he cannot read and the girl tells him it is a bookmark. Huck goes towards the river, wondering what this is all about, and the Negro told to look after him catches him up and asks him to go to the swamp. There Huck finds Jim hiding – the Grangerford slaves have been looking after him ever since he managed to swim ashore. He has been buying in supplies and mending their raft. But before they can make plans, events take a violent turn. Huck gets up the next day to find the house deserted. Miss Sophia has eloped with Harney Shepherdson and the note Huck carried between them was to complete the arrangements. The whole Grangerford clan has turned out to hunt down Sophia's lover and kill him. Even the women 'has gone for to stir up de relations' (p. 173)

An Account of the Plot: **Chapter 19, pp. 177–86**

and the men have ridden out with their guns. Huck hides in a tree overlooking the woodstore by the steamboat landing and sees the later stages of the battle. Mr Shepherdson and his two older sons have been killed already. Huck manages to have a brief conversation with Buck (p. 174), who is wounded almost immediately afterwards, together with his cousin Joe. The two boys jump into the river while the Shepherdsons run along the bank, shouting, 'Kill them, kill them!' (p. 175). Huck is revolted by the carnage and finds it too sickening to describe. 'I wished I hadn't ever come ashore that night, to see such things' (p. 175). He stays up his tree until the shooting is over. When he comes down, he sees the two boys' bodies lying at the water-edge. He pulls them ashore and sorrowfully covers their faces. 'I cried a little when I was covering up Buck's face, for he was mighty good to me' (p. 175). Huck feels to blame for the slaughter, which resulted from the note he carried between Miss Sophia and Harney Shepherdson. These two have now escaped across the river. Huck looks for Jim in the swamp but cannot find him. He finds him by the raft, waiting to hear for certain whether Huck has been killed in the fight. They have a joyful reunion and set out once more down the Mississippi. 'We said there warn't no home like a raft, after all. Other places do seem so cramped up and smothery, but a raft don't' (p. 176).

These two chapters on the Grangerfords should be taken together as a unit. By the time he wrote them, Twain's nostalgia for the old South of his boyhood had been considerably modified by his adult views on slavery and the violence that he saw as inbred into the Southern code of honour. The two chapters are a savage denunciation of the reality lying behind all the romance and chivalry. (Compare with any films or TV serials you may have seen with the same setting.)

CHAPTER 19, pp. 177–86

The opening pages of this chapter contain some of the finest descriptive passages in the book. Huck's and Jim's life on the river is an idyllic picture of man in harmony with nature. Huck once more quickly recovers from the violence he has witnessed. But this contented existence is not to last very long. One morning, Huck finds another canoe and he paddles ashore for berries. He sees two men fleeing from a crowd of angry pursuers. One is about thirty, the other about seventy upwards. Huck rescues them and they breakfast with Huck and Jim among the cottonwood trees. They are confidence men whose tricks for cheating people out of their money have been found out. The self-reliance and versatility that were so admired as American virtues are satirized in the two men's list of skills: the younger has worked as printer, quack-doctor, actor, lecturer, teacher, phrenologist and mesmerist – 'most anything that comes handy, so it ain't work' (p. 182); the older is a faith-healer, fortune teller, preacher and missionary. The younger man claims to be the rightful Duke of Bridgewater and insists on being waited on and being called 'your Grace'. Jim and Huck are sorry for him, so try to comfort him by falling in with his wishes. The old man becomes jealous of 'all that petting' and tells them that he is 'the pore disappeared Dauphin ... son of Looy the Sixteen and Marry Antonette' (p. 184), the lawful King of France. After a spell of acting 'huffy' at being so outwitted, the duke accepts the king's offer of friendship. Jim and Huck are 'pretty glad to see it ... for what you want ... on a raft, is for everybody to be satisfied, and feel right and kind towards the others' (p. 185). Huck of course is not deceived: he knows the two are 'low-down humbugs and frauds', but he has learned from his experience with Pap 'that the best way to get along with his kind of people is to let them have their own way' in order to 'keep peace in the family' (p. 186). He does not tell Jim that these two are not what they claim to be. Unfortunately Huck's attempt to restore harmony on the raft is not going to succeed. The corruption of the shore has invaded it. The entry of the king and the duke mark the end of one stage of the story. From now on, whole communities will be satirized: their cruelty and stupidity will be shown up in the way the two rogues manage to exploit them. The king and the duke are among Twain's finest comic characters.

CHAPTER 20, pp. 187–96

The hypocrisy and delusions of the shore have now taken over the raft. The newcomers ask awkward questions about Jim. Huck spins another tall yarn to make them believe that Jim is his own property and to give a convincing reason for not travelling by daylight. This of course is very inconvenient for the king and duke. Good-naturedly, Huck and Jim allow them to take their beds in the wigwam. After a stormy night the king instructs the duke on how to play a scene from *Romeo and Juliet*. Huck lands with them at Pokeville (town name on p. 194), which is 'a little one-horse town about three mile down the bend' (p. 191), where the duke looks for a printer's office. Huck goes with the king to a camp-meeting (an emotional religious gathering), which has drawn an audience from twenty miles around. The king pretends to be a reformed pirate; he works so enthusiastically at this role that he collects over eighty dollars in donations and steals a three-gallon jug of whisky on his way back to the raft. The duke has made some money too from his use of the unattended printing press. He has also run off a poster describing Jim as a runaway slave. This will allow them to travel down the river by day. If they meet anyone, they will tie Jim up and say they are taking him back to his owners for the reward. Jim submits but hopes that he and Huck will not 'run acrost any mo' kings on dis trip . . . I doan mine one er two kings, but dat's enough' (p. 196).

The camp-meeting is one of the many amusing crowd-scenes in the second half of *The Adventures of Huckleberry Finn*. Here Twain is once more satirizing false piety: the townspeople have lost touch with reality and love empty words so much that they are easily fooled by the king.

CHAPTER 21, pp. 197–207

The next day the king and duke suffer from a hangover – 'pretty rusty' is the way Huck describes them (p. 197). They practise their Shakespeare scenes and the duke teaches the king Hamlet's soliloquy 'To be, or not to be' – or, rather, his own unique version, which is 'a barrel of odds and ends' from several plays (p. 198). A few days later they land at Bricksville in Arkansaw. (This, like all the little towns along the river, is based on Twain's native Hannibal.) A touring circus has already reached the town, so they are assured of a good audience. The duke hires the court house for their performance and Huck accompanies the two actors as they go round the town sticking up play-bills (p. 200). The town is full of bored loafers, whose only diversions are drinking, chewing tobacco and tormenting animals. Huck sees three fights as he goes round the town. An old man called Boggs rides in for his 'little old monthly drunk' (p. 203). He is 'yelling like an Injun' and 'weaving about in his saddle'. Boggs makes a habit of uttering loud-mouthed threats; and this time he has 'come to town to kill old Colonel Sherburn' (p. 204). The spectators are amused as Boggs rides up to Sherburn's store. 'He don't mean nothing . . . He's the best-naturedest old fool in Arkansaw – never hurt nobody, drunk nor sober' (p. 204). The laughter is silenced when Sherburn steps out and warns Boggs not to continue his 'blackguarding' after one o'clock. The drunken Boggs, full of bravado, keeps on taunting Sherburn, despite the efforts of the crowd to drag him away. Eventually he is too drunk either to shout or even stand up. When Sherburn reappears and stands with his pistol cocked, Boggs calls out for mercy. Sherburn shoots Boggs just as Boggs's daughter is running along the street. Scornfully, Sherburn throws down his pistol and walks away; the crowd first takes the dying Boggs to a drugstore and then jostles for a sight of his body. One man mimes the whole scene over again and is treated to several drinks. But the mood of the crowd changes quickly; someone says that Sherburn ought to be lynched and they set out with washing-lines to carry out his suggestion.

There is a deliberate parallel between the acting rehearsals at the beginning of the chapter and the violence that breaks out at the end. The crowd treat the murder like a theatrical performance put on to while away their boredom. They do try to make Boggs behave more prudently; but once the drama is under way, their reactions are callous: they push and shove each other to get a glimpse of the body and they applaud the man who reenacts the murder. Their detachment is reflected in the way the murder is described. The attitudes of Boggs and Sherburn, confronting each other in the street, are 'stagey'; Sherburn 'was standing perfectly still . . . the pistol barrel come down slow and steady to a level – both barrels cocked' (p. 205). Even the young girl throwing herself across her father's body is in the approved style of melodrama. We feel that the people are not really sorry for Boggs or his daughter. In turning against Sherburn, they are only searching for more amusement. It is part of Twain's skill as a writer that he can use this device and still make us feel horrified as we see Boggs change from a drunken buffoon to a pathetic and frightened old man, shot down in cold blood.

CHAPTER 22, pp. 208-13

The crowd streams towards Sherburn's house, 'whooping and yelling' (p. 208), and tears down the fence round his yard. Sherburn comes out with a shotgun and the crowd is intimidated. Sherburn laughs in a way 'that makes you feel like when you are eating bread that's got sand in it' (p. 208). He speaks to the crowd with withering contempt, telling them they have the kind of courage that can rise to tarring and feathering 'poor friendless cast-out women' (p. 209), but that is never up to a real fight. As Sherburn cocks his gun, the crowd scatters and flees. Huck sneaks into the circus by ducking under the tent flap. He is astonished at the skill of the bareback riders and delighted by the clown. Another clown, posing as a drunk, insists on joining the act. Huck is fooled like the rest of the audience, which is roaring with laughter at the man's 'attempts' to keep his balance on the horse and stay upright. Huck holds his breath for the safety of the 'drunk': 'It warn't funny to me, though; I was all of a tremble to see his danger' (p. 212). Suddenly the man stands erect on the saddle and throws off layer after layer of clothing, until he stands there 'slim and handsome, and dressed the gaudiest and prettiest you ever saw' (p. 212). The clown exits to thunderous applause from the delighted audience. Huck feels 'sheepish' at being fooled in this way, but sorrier for the ringmaster, not realizing that the whole act is a put-up 'stunt'. In contrast, the show put on by the king and duke attracts only twelve people. The duke quickly changes the programme to 'low comedy' and advertises it with the warning 'Ladies and children not admitted'. He says, 'If that line don't fetch them, I don't know Arkansaw!' (p. 213).

This chapter and the last express Twain's harsh judgement on the world of his boyhood. At first, Chapter 22 may seem strangely constructed: it gives the second half of an incident begun in the previous chapter (Colonel Sherburn and Boggs) and then describes two more quite separate incidents. But the arrangement is deliberate: the townsfolk are made to show themselves up discreditably in three quite separate ways. They are violent but cowardly when one person stands up to them; they are taken in by showy illusions (the circus); and, lastly, they can be drawn by low comedy, particularly if there is a hint of obscenity to it (see note 2. on pp. 390–91). Most of the incidents are based on real events that happened in or near Hannibal, Missouri, during Twain's boyhood.

CHAPTER 23, pp. 214–19

This chapter describes the confidence trick played on the all-male audience at Bricksville. The tragedy of 'The King's Camelopard or the Royal Nonesuch' consists of the king, painted in stripes, leaping about naked on the stage, on all fours. The audience are amused and clap for more; but their laughter turns to rage when they realize that this is all there is to the performance. Not wanting to be laughed at, they keep their mouths shut about the deception and there is another full house on the following night. On the third night, Huck notices that the audience files in with their pockets full of refuse and with dead cats (to pelt at the stage). The duke makes someone else stand at the door for him and slips back to the raft with Huck. The king has not even left the raft. They cast off and do not light a fire until they are ten miles below the village. 'Greenhorns, flatheads!' exults the duke (p. 216). They have made two hundred and sixty-five dollars. While the two rogues sleep, Jim expresses his surprise at their behaviour: they are 'reglar rapscallions' (p. 216). Huck says that this is the way all royalty behaves and quotes some muddled examples from history to prove that 'all kings is mostly rapscallions' (p. 216). The next morning, Jim is depressed and homesick for his wife and children. Wonderingly, Huck comments, 'I do believe he cared just as much for his people as white folks does for their'n. It don't seem natural, but I reckon it's so' (p. 218). Jim tells Huck about an incident when his daughter had appeared to disobey him, after he told her to shut the door. He had hit the little girl – and then suddenly realized that she had gone deaf after a recent attack of scarlet fever: 'De Lord God Amighty fogive po' ole Jim, kaze he never gwyne to fogive hisself as long's he live!' (p. 219).

This chapter shows Twain's belief in the similarity between real kings and aristocracy and their counterfeits, the king and the duke. The behaviour of these scoundrels and their dupes is strongly contrasted with Jim's anguish as he remembers hitting his little daughter. Note that Huck is sympathetic; but his conditioning still makes him think it surprising that a Negro slave should have the same feelings as 'white folks'.

CHAPTER 24, pp. 220–26

The voyage down the river continues and they reach a place where there is a village on each bank. Jim complains about having to be tied up for several hours every day to make the story of his being a recaptured slave more authentic. The duke disguises him as a 'Sick Arab' in a King Lear costume and leaves him free; then the duke and king separate, intending each to 'work' one of the two villages. All of them, including Huck, put on smarter clothes. The king asks Huck to paddle for three miles up above the village, so that they can catch a steamboat and appear to arrive in style from one of the large towns up river. On the way, they pick up a 'nice innocent-looking young country jake' (p. 221), who gossips to them about the death of Peter Wilks, a wealthy local tanner, after a long illness. His two brothers have already been summoned from England. Posing as a preacher, the king skilfully extracts more facts about the Wilkses. When he finds that the young man is on his way to South America, the king moves swiftly into action. He gets Huck to fetch the duke; he wants the three of them to land at the village from another steamboat, claiming to be the dead man's brothers, with Huck as their valet. The king puts on an English accent; 'Bilgewater', as the king calls him, has to pretend to be deaf and dumb. When they land, and are told that their 'brother' is dead, the king and the duke pretend to be overcome with grief. '. . . both of them took on about that dead tanner like they'd lost the twelve disciples. Well, if ever I struck anything like it, I'm a nigger. It was enough to make a body ashamed of the human race.' (p. 226).

Here we see another form of the confidence trick – the skilful use of an opportunity that turns up unexpectedly. Huck once more goes along with the deception, but for the first time he shows some disgust at what the rogues are doing.

CHAPTER 25, pp. 227–34

The whole village turns out to see the king and the duke arrive at their 'brother's' house, where the dead man's three nieces are waiting for them – Mary Jane, Susan and Joanna. The king and the duke go to look at the body lying in its coffin. They 'bust out a crying . . . and . . . put their arms around each other's necks' (pp. 227–8) and work on the crowd with their sham grief until everyone else is 'sobbing right out loud' (p. 228). Huck dismisses all this, in a famous phrase, as 'soul-butter and hogwash' (p. 228). The king adds to his performance by being able to name the dead man's friends, whom he invites to supper. Huck consider Mr Wilks's neighbours a 'passel of sapheads' (p. 229) for being taken in by all this pretence. (The duke has to pretend to be deaf and dumb, so he merely makes signs, and gurgles.) The dead man has left a letter, dividing his property between his nieces and his brothers. Harvey and William – the brothers – are to get half of the six thousand dollars in gold which is hidden in the cellar. Finding that the sum is short by four hundred and fifteen dollars, the king and the duke make up the sum themselves. They return upstairs, where the king says that he cannot rob the 'poor sweet lambs' (p. 231). He asks his 'nieces' to take the whole amount. This impresses the neighbours even more. The king gets carried away by his eloquence, in a long speech about his 'brother's' funeral 'orgies', and is spotted as a fraud by Dr Robinson, a friend of Peter Wilks, who has come in late. He tries to warn Mary Jane that she and her sisters are being deceived by 'the thinnest kind of an impostor' (p. 234) and begs her to turn the king out. Her response is to hand over the whole sum of money to the king and ask him to invest it for herself and her sisters. 'Everybody clapped their hands and stomped on the floor like a perfect storm' (p. 234). The doctor goes off, saying he washes his hands of the matter. His parting remark is given a witty reply by the king and the audience consider it 'a prime good hit' (p. 234).

Twain pokes savage fun at the gullibility of the people at this village and plainly implies that if they had not been so corrupted by false emotion, they would have seen through the imposters. Twain himself was strongly anti-Christian: that is, he loathed the structures of organized religion and was deeply suspicious of the almost hysterical emotion associated with 'camp-meetings'. He felt that the behaviour of Southern society made nonsense of the religious values it professed to believe in.

CHAPTER 26, pp. 235–43

So far, Huck has been a passive spectator of the trick being played on the Wilks family. Soon he is forced into giving the conmen active support. He is having supper with the youngest sister, Joanna, and she questions him about his life in England. Huck's replies make Joanna even more doubtful but she is scolded by her sisters for being unkind to a guest. They tell her to ask Huck's pardon and 'she done it beautiful' (p. 240). Huck now feels 'ornery and low down and mean' (p. 240) for standing by while the girls are robbed of their money and wants to do something to foil the king and duke. He decides that the only safe way is to steal the money, hide it and write a note after he has left the neighbourhood to reveal where it is hidden. He goes up to the king's room but as he has to search in the dark his first attempt to find the money is unsuccessful. He overhears the king and the duke talking as he stands behind a curtain. The duke is uneasy about the doctor: they should 'clip it down the river' (p. 241) with what they have gained already. The king jeers at such cowardice: he wants to stay until they have had time to auction off the girls' property, which will raise another eight or nine thousand dollars. He crushes the duke's slight qualms about such wholesale robbery by pointing out that the auction will not be legal once they are found out and 'it'll all go back to the estate' (p. 242), while the king and the duke will still have their money from the sale. Nothing can go wrong with their plan – they have 'all the fools in town' on their side (p. 242). Huck watches them hide the money in a mattress and when they have left, he takes it up to his own room.

We see here that Huck's morality is based on a strong personal response to human suffering and a wish to help people who have been kind to him, rather than on any abstract set of rules. He has seen people being duped by the impostors before and not felt obliged to intervene. Huck's own tall stories have so far been told to help him survive and not for gain; now he is ashamed to be helping prop up the lies that are being told to the Wilks girls.

CHAPTER 27, pp. 244–51

That night Huck looks for a place downstairs to hide the gold. He is disturbed by Mary Jane and hurriedly puts the bag of gold into the coffin. In the morning, there is a public viewing of the body organized by the undertaker – one of Twain's finest brief character-sketches. Huck has not time to verify the gold is still where he put it before the undertaker seals the coffin (p. 247). After the funeral, the king announces that he has to return to his congregation in England. He delights everyone by saying that he and his brother will take the girls home with them. Next day, however, the neighbours are shocked when the king sells the Negro slaves, splitting up their families (p. 248). The duke becomes uneasy but the king still insists on remaining until they have auctioned off the property. The next day, they discover that the gold has disappeared from the mattress and cross-question Huck. He pretends that he has seen some Negroes creeping into the king's room and the two scoundrels think the gold has been taken away by the slaves they sold. The duke is quite amused but the king is furious. Huck feels pleased that he has 'worked it all off onto the niggers and yet hadn't done the niggers no harm by it' (p. 251).

By now Huck's skill at surviving in river society has reached such a pitch that he can outcheat even such conmen as the king and duke. The most important incident is the grief of the Wilks sisters when they hear that their slaves are to be sold. We remember that it was a similar incident that caused Jim to run away. Note too that although the townspeople are indignant at this act of cruelty, they do not try to stop the sale; they do not question their own assumptions that the Negroes can be treated as disposable property.

CHAPTER 28, pp. 252–62

Huck feels 'awful bad' when he finds Mary Jane weeping bitterly over the fate of the slaves. The excitement of a journey to England has been completely spoiled for her. Before he can stop himself, Huck has reassured her that the Negroes will not be separated after all; and the girl's relief and delight make Huck decide to tell her the truth. His reasons for doing this show once again that Huck lives from minute to minute and does not act on any fixed principle: '. . . I reckon a body that ups and tells the truth when he is in a tight place, is taking considerable many resks . . . and yet here's a case where I'm blest if it don't look to me like the truth is better, and actuly *safer*, than a lie' (pp. 252–3). He explains to Mary Jane that 'these uncles of yourn' are a couple of frauds. Mary Jane wants to have them tarred and feathered; but Huck says that if she 'blows' on them at once, he will be all right but someone else – meaning Jim – will be 'in big trouble' (p. 254). He persuades her to go away for a few days, so that she will not have to face the king and duke, and to let the auction go ahead. He sends her off with a note which explains where he has hidden the gold and then makes up another story for Susan and Joanna. In the middle of the auction a steamboat arrives, bringing the genuine Wilks brothers.

Huck's ingenuity has now brought about such a tangle of misunderstanding that it seems impossible for it ever to be unravelled. He says proudly, '. . . I reckoned Tom Sawyer couldn't a done it no neater himself' (p. 261). The only person who knows the truth, apart from Huck, has been sent away. But the situation is abruptly simplified by the arrival of the true heirs.

CHAPTER 29, pp. 263–73

Huck admires the coolness of the king and duke, confronted by Peter Wilks's real brothers. No doubt the two rogues have had plenty of practice in dealing with this kind of emergency. Even Huck notices that the new arrivals' accent sounds more genuinely English but the king pours scorn on Harvey and William Wilks; how convenient that their baggage has been mislaid, so that they cannot identify themselves, and the dumb brother (William) cannot make signs because he has broken his arm! The crowd sides with the king and duke but Dr Robinson and a lawyer, Levi Bell, are suspicious, as is a man who claims to have seen the king and duke travelling in the canoe with Huck. The doctor suggests that the two sets of brothers should be taken to the local tavern for a series of questions and tests. There, he asks the king to produce the bag of gold; the king says that it has been stolen by the Negroes. Huck finds himself forced to support this story. The doctor and lawyer 'grill' the king but they let Huck off lightly, realizing that he is not a hardened conman like the other two. The king fails a writing test set by the lawyer but manages to find an excuse. The real Harvey Wilks challenges him to describe the tattoo on his brother's breast and the king says it is 'a small, thin, blue arrow' (p. 269). When Harvey contradicts him, the men who laid out the body cannot remember seeing any mark at all. The spectators have almost decided to drown 'the whole *bilin*'' as frauds, when the lawyer suggests that they should dig up the body. A storm is brewing but the excited crowd drags Huck and the four claimants along the river bank 'just carrying on like wild-cats' (p. 270) and shouting that they will 'lynch the whole gang' if they do not find the tattoo mark on the corpse. Amid rain and lightning the crowd swarms over Peter Wilks's grave and begins to dig up his coffin. As they unscrew the lid, a blinding flash reveals the bag of gold hidden in the coffin by Huck. In the rush to get at it, Huck escapes. He manages to find a canoe and paddles back to the raft, calling out to Jim to cast off: '. . . in two seconds, away we went, a sliding down the river, and it *did* seem so good to be free again . . . and nobody to bother us' (pp. 272–3). But he is congratulating himself too soon – very shortly he sees the king and duke 'making their skiff hum' and the two rogues climb aboard again.

This chapter provides the climax to the whole Wilks episode. Notice the superb skill with which the suspense builds up, as the king and duke wriggle out of one awkward situation after another. The black humour of the graveyard scene, where the frenzied crowd desecrates

Peter Wilks's coffin, is one of Twain's most powerful attacks on small-town society. The hysteria of the crowd is mirrored by the unleashed violence of the storm in which the scene takes place. Huck accepts the return of the king and duke with resigned fatalism: '... I wilted right down onto the planks, then, and give up' (p. 273).

CHAPTER 30, pp. 274–7

A short tail-piece to the last section. Huck lies his way out when the king accuses him of trying to give them the slip. There is a quarrel between the two conmen, each accusing the other of intending to steal the gold for himself. The king, usually more quick-witted than the duke, has to give way before the brute strength of the younger man. They make up their differences over a drink and when they are asleep, Huck tells Jim what happened ashore.

CHAPTER 31, pp. 278–87

The raft has now drifted eleven hundred miles down the river (p. 366) and has reached the deep South. The king and duke try out their stock of tricks round the villages but this time meet with little success. They begin to whisper together; Jim and Huck think they must be planning 'worse deviltry than ever' (p. 278) and decide they must break away from them for good. One day the king goes ashore at a place named Pikesville, telling the others to 'stay hid' while he finds out whether it is safe to play the Royal Nonesuch. The duke and Huck follow later and find the king creating a drunken scene in a bar. The two men begin to squabble, so Huck seizes his chance and runs back to the raft. Jim has disappeared. Huck sits down and cries; but when he sets out along the road (p. 280), he meets a boy from whom he learns that the king has used the 'reward' notice (see p. 195) to con a farmer called Silas Phelps into buying his share of the reward for forty dollars. Jim has been handed over to the farmer, who hopes to claim two hundred dollars from Jim's imaginary owner at the St Jaques' plantation. Huck returns to the raft to think out what he must do, now that everything is 'all busted up and ruined' (p. 281). He is faced not just with a difficult practical problem; he has to deal with the severest moral test he has yet encountered. Huck is a product of Southern society. He has rejected that society's conventions of behaviour but not its inbred belief in slavery. How deeply and subtly this belief is rooted – even in such an outcast as Huck – is shown by the way his thoughts run. Since Jim has to be a 'slave again all his life', would he not be better off at home with Miss Watson? But if he writes to Miss Watson, she might treat Jim badly for being so 'ungrateful' as to run away from her. Besides, 'it would get all around that Huck Finn helped a nigger to get his freedom' (p. 281). If anybody found that out, Huck would 'be ready to get down and lick his boots for shame'. Huck sees this dilemma as his punishment for helping Jim to escape in the first place, instead of letting Miss Watson know where he was. Suddenly he realizes 'that here was the plain hand of Providence . . . letting me know my wickedness was being watched all the time from up there in heaven' (p. 281). Huck becomes concerned about the state of his soul and the danger of 'everlasting fire' and he tries to pray to see if he can 'quit being the kind of a boy' he is; but the words will not come. He isn't 'square'; he is 'playing double' (p.282) – that is, he knows 'you can't pray a lie', because he is not sincere in his intentions to 'write to that nigger's owner'. Huck decides to write the letter first and pray afterwards. 'Glad and excited', he writes a short note to tell Miss Watson that Jim is at Phelps's farm. Immediately he feels 'good and all washed clean of sin for the first time' in his life. But as he looks at the letter, thinking how near he came to 'being lost and going to hell' (p. 283), he begins to remember Jim's kindness to him and the happy times they have had on the raft. His love for Jim overwhelms him: 'I was a trembling, because I'd got to decide, forever, betwixt two things . . . I studied a minute, sort of holding my breath, and then says to myself: "All right, then, I'll *go* to hell" – and tore it up' (p. 283).

This decision that Huck takes – when he rejects his Southern conditioning and his heart defeats his 'conscience' – is the climax of the whole book. The whole passage is deliberately ironic. Twain is showing us that in a corrupt society evil becomes good and good evil. The fact that Huck still thinks that what he is doing is wrong is the strongest condemnation of Southern values.

After deciding that he will 'steal Jim out of slavery again' (p. 283), next day Huck hides the raft and canoe and sets out for Phelps's farm. He takes a roundabout route, going past it to the town, as he wants to make it appear that he is coming from that direction. He runs into the duke and pretends that the raft has been lost. The duke is anxious to get rid of Huck and says that Jim has been sold to a man who lives forty miles away. Huck pretends to set out in this direction but when he is out of sight of the duke doubles back towards the farm.

CHAPTER 32, pp. 288–94

Phelps's farm is 'one of those little one-horse cotton plantations' (p. 288) and Huck describes it in detail. As he approaches the living-quarters, a pack of dogs surrounds him. A Negro woman comes out when she hears the noise and then Mrs Phelps herself. She seizes Huck, and hugs him, and addresses him as 'Tom', telling him to call her 'Aunt Sally'. Huck falls into the role but almost immediately is 'up a stump' (p. 292), as he knows nothing about the family background his 'aunt' talks about. He is saved by the return of Silas Phelps; for the past few days he has been making regular trips to the steamboat landing, hoping to meet his nephew. Mrs Phelps makes Huck hide behind a bed and teases her husband for several minutes before she pulls Huck out of his hiding-place. Neither Mr nor Mrs Phelps has seen their nephew before. When the farmer asks, 'Why, who's that?' (p. 293), Mrs Phelps tells him (and Huck), 'It's *Tom Sawyer*!' Huck is of course filled with relief: 'it was like being born again, I was so glad to find out who I was' (p. 293). Huck is now able to give all the details they want about 'his' family. Realizing that the real Tom Sawyer may arrive at any moment, he says he must go back to town to collect his baggage and sets out in the wagon to intercept his friend.

The almost incredible coincidence that saves Huck from being found out sets the tone for the final section of the novel. Many

52 *Passnotes:* **The Adventures of Huckleberry Finn**

readers have found it an anti-climax, after the serious issues dealt with in the middle chapters (see 'The Ending of *The Adventures of Huckleberry Finn*', p. 91). Huck's feelings of melancholy as he approaches the farm are similar to his mood in the opening pages and may perhaps be explained as an instinctive knowledge that civilization is closing round him again. The farm is based on the one belonging to John Quarles, Mark Twain's uncle, which the writer often visited when he was a boy. Notice particularly Aunt Sally's conversation with Huck about the grounded steamboat (p. 291); '"Anybody hurt?" "No'm. Killed a nigger." "Well, it's lucky; because sometimes people do get hurt."' What point is Twain making here and why does it come so soon after Huck's decision to 'go to hell' for Jim?

CHAPTER 33, pp. 295–302

Huck meets Tom Sawyer half-way to town. At first Tom thinks that Huck is a ghost. Huck explains part of what has happened to him and promises to tell the rest later. Tom at once takes charge; he hands his own luggage over to Huck and tells him to go back to the farm with it; he (Tom) will arrive later, pretending to be a stranger. Huck tells Tom that Jim is being held by the Phelpses; and says, defensively, that he is planning to set Jim free. To his astonishment, Tom wants to help: '... I'm bound to say, Tom Sawyer fell, considerable, in my estimation ... Tom Sawyer a *nigger stealer*!' (p. 296). Huck's early return from town is put down to the speed of the mare drawing the wagon. Half an hour later, Tom walks in, pretending to be mistaken about the name of the farm. He is invited to dinner, in the middle of which he kisses Aunt Sally on the mouth – much to her indignation, as she does not know he is her nephew. Tom plays with the situation a little longer and then passes himself off as his own brother Sid – another character from *The Adventures of Tom Sawyer*. During the afternoon Tom and Huck try to find out where Jim is being kept locked up but are unsuccessful. At supper, one of the Phelps children asks to be allowed to go with the two visitors to a 'show' in town. (This is the Royal Nonesuch.) Uncle Silas refuses. He has been told by Jim that the show is a fraud and the townspeople are going to drive the 'owdacious loafers' (p. 301) – the king and the duke – out of town. Despite the way the king and duke have treated him, Huck wants to warn them. He and Tom climb out of their bedroom window and secretly make their way into town. They arrive at about half past eight and run into a 'raging rush of people, with torches . . . banging tin pans and blowing horns . . . they had the king and the duke astraddle of a rail . . . all over tar and feathers . . . like a couple of monstrous big soldier-plumes' (p. 301). Huck's natural kindness and compassion are shown by his comments on the mob's behaviour: '. . . I was sorry for them poor pitiful rascals . . . It was a dreadful thing to see. Human beings *can* be awful cruel to one another' (pp. 301–2). He even feels 'to blame, somehow' (p. 302). Already, however, in this chapter we can see Huck's direct contact with the world is beginning to give way before Tom's childish tricks. Tom's unfinished sentence (p. 296) – 'What! Why Jim is –' – is a 'plant' for one of the revelations in the last chapter.

CHAPTER 34, pp. 303–9

On the way home Tom manages to work out where Jim is being held; he has noticed food being taken over to one of the huts. Huck has a simple plan for releasing Jim and getting him away from the farm. For Tom it is 'too blame' simple (p. 304). He puts forward another scheme which Huck admits is 'worth fifteen of mine, for style', although he knows that details will change before it is put into effect. They go over to the hut and find that it has a window that Jim could easily climb out of; but Tom insists that they must dig Jim out through the lean-to beside the hut, as this will prolong his escape: 'It'll take about a week!' (p. 306). In the morning they go down to the Negro cabins and make friends with Nat (p. 321), the slave who is feeding Jim. His hair is 'all tied up in little bunches with thread' to keep off the witches. Nat takes the boys to visit Jim and is astonished when Jim cries out a greeting. Tom manages to convince Nat that the witches made him imagine all this and Nat begs him not to mention that he is 'witched' in case the Phelpses punish him. Tom gives him a dime and, when Nat steps out of the dark hut to examine it, he tells

54 *Passnotes: The Adventures of Huckleberry Finn*

Jim to keep pretending that he does not know them. He also warns him to take no notice of any digging sounds he may hear by night. Nat is so afraid of the witches that he will be glad to have company at any time he has to enter the hut to feed Jim.

This chapter introduces a lengthy set of incidents in which Tom will persuade Jim to cooperate in playing out his escape fantasies, all copied from novels of romantic adventure. Several critics feel that the slapstick humour of this last section diminishes both the relationship that has grown up between Jim and Huck and their own status as characters – Huck fading out altogether and Jim being pulled back into the insulting role of the 'comic Negro'. There has been great disagreement about Twain's intentions from Chapter 34 onwards. Some ways of assessing your own reactions will be suggested in the final section of these notes.

CHAPTER 35, pp. 310–17

Tom is annoyed at the casual way that Jim is kept locked up, while the Phelpses wait for his owners to claim him. It is 'so rotten difficult to get up a difficult plan' (p. 310). There is no watchman or dog to be drugged, Jim's chain could easily be slipped off his bed-post, and the key to the hut is easily accessible. Tom puts a lot of energy into making his escape plan as complicated as possible; he keeps on rejecting Huck's common-sense suggestions. The boys take various articles from the house, including three case-knives. Tom insists that they must use these to dig Jim out, although there are digging tools lying near by.

See the Notes pp. 392–3 for explanation of the heroic figures mentioned by Tom. One of them is the famous Count of Monte Cristo, central figure of the classic romantic story of escape and revenge by Dumas. Twain believed that such works were responsible for holding back the entry of the South into the modern world.

CHAPTER 36, pp. 318–23

That night, Tom and Huck dig for several hours with the case-knives, making very little progress and blistering their hands. Although 'it ain't moral', Tom grudgingly admits that they will have to use proper digging tools but they must pretend that they are case-knives. When Huck says that he doesn't 'care shucks for the morality of it, nohow', and will use 'the handiest thing', Tom replies: 'It might answer for *you* to dig Jim out with a pick, *without* any letting-on, because you don't know no better; but it wouldn't for me, because I do know better' (p. 319). After two bouts of digging with pick and shovel they break into Jim's hut. On lighting a candle they are relieved to find Jim 'hearty and healthy'. Jim is overjoyed: 'He was so glad to see us, he most cried' (p. 320). He wants to leave as soon as possible. Tom says this is 'unregular'; he tells Jim 'all about our plans, and how we could alter them in a minute any time there was an alarm' (p. 321). Jim agrees and Tom says he will send in a 'rope-ladder pie' through Nat. Tom tells Huck this is 'the best fun he ever had in his life . . . if he only could see his way to it we would keep it up all the rest of our lives and leave Jim to our children to get out' (pp. 321–2). On one visit the boys forget to shut the door of the lean-to; eleven dogs wriggle in through the hole they have made. Nat thinks the witches are after him again and Tom promises to send in a 'witch-pie' to feed them if Nat will promise not to look at the pie or touch its contents.

Tom is now so obsessed by his fantasies that he has no thought for the suffering he may cause. He has already frightened the muddle-headed Nat and dashed Jim's hopes of instant freedom. Are we meant to find these incidents amusing or is Twain trying to show us that the Southern love of 'dreams and phantoms' corrupts even its juvenile members? Another facet of the complex attitude to slavery is shown: Aunt Sally and Uncle Silas are taking a personal interest in Jim and feeding him well – but their concern for him does not stop them from locking him up. And, naturally, they do not question the fact that he must be returned to his owner.

CHAPTER 37, pp. 324–30

The boys continue to 'smouch' things from the house. They hide a spoon in Uncle Silas's coat pocket and a nail in his hat. Jim is supposed to steal these when Mr Phelps next visits him. A sheet and a shirt also disappear. Tom and Huck confuse Aunt Sally by making objects vanish and appear again, until she is too bewildered to continue counting. The rope pie is difficult to bake, until Tom and Huck come across a warming pan in the attic and take it out to the woods. After a number of balked attempts they 'turned out a pie that was a satisfaction to look at' (p. 330). The sheet has been torn into strands and made into a rope which has been baked inside the pie.

Huck falls meekly in with Tom's plans, which have now drawn in both Aunt Sally and Uncle Silas. Huck's remarks about Mr Phelps's bewilderment on finding some rat-holes already stopped up (p. 327) may perhaps be taken as a subdued criticism of Tom's self-centred absorption in his 'fun': 'And so he went on a mumbling up stairs, and then we left. He was a mighty nice old man. And always is.'

CHAPTER 38, pp. 331–7

Tom decides that Jim cannot escape before he has scribbled an inscription and his coat of arms on the prison wall. He reels off a number of heraldic terms, which he cannot explain to Jim and Huck. Unable to decide which of the inscriptions he likes best, Tom says that they must all be used; and, as Jim cannot write, Tom will block out the words for him to follow: 'they don't have log walls in a dungeon', so the words must be written on a stone especially brought in – 'a gaudy big grindstone down at the mill' (p. 333). The height of absurdity is reached when the two boys find the stone is too heavy for them and they are forced to let Jim out of the cabin to help them trundle it back. Tom then suggests that Jim must have a pet – a spider, rat or rattlesnake would be suitable for taming. He also wants Jim to raise a flower and water it with his tears. At Jim's unenthusiastic response '... Tom most lost all patience with him ... So Jim he was sorry, and said he wouldn't behave so no more' (p. 337).

By now the story has been taken over completely by farce and practical jokes. Compare this and the first half of the next chapter with the earlier incident (Chapter 10) when Jim is bitten by a rattlesnake.

CHAPTER 39, pp. 338–43

Tom and Huck collect spiders, rats and snakes for Jim's hut. The snakes (which are harmless) manage to escape and swarm round the house, greatly distressing Aunt Sally. Despite being beaten, the boys make another collection and Jim endures the company of his 'pets' for three weeks. By this time, Uncle Silas has written several times to the plantation from which Jim has supposedly escaped and has received no reply. Mr Phelps decides to advertise Jim in the New Orleans and St Louis papers. This alarms Huck (in case they are read by anyone in St Petersburg) and Tom says it is time to send the 'nonnamous' letters to warn people that Jim is about to escape. He makes Huck dress up as a servant-girl to push a note under the door: '*Beware. Trouble is brewing. Keep a sharp lookout*. UNKNOWN FRIEND' (p. 342). Tom also draws pictures in blood on the outside doors and the Phelpses become so nervous that they post servants by the doors to sit up all night. Tom writes a much longer letter informing his aunt and uncle that 'a desprate gang of cutthroats' is going to steal Jim that night (p. 343). He finds one of the guards asleep at his post and sticks the letter 'in the back of his neck'.

We see that Tom is so wrapped up in his own imagination that he cannot understand what will happen if he tries to involve the adults in his games: 'if we don't *give* them notice, there won't be nobody nor nothing to interfere with us, and so after all our hard work and trouble this escape'll go off perfectly flat' (p. 341). Yet in the 1840s (the supposed time of the action), this part of the United States was still frontier territory and the settlers were constantly on the alert against gangs of armed men that roamed about it. Reality is about to break in on Tom's romantic 'evasion' plans.

CHAPTER 40, pp. 344–50

The boys have a day's fishing on the river; when they return they find the adults in a state of 'sweat and worry' (p. 344). The boys are sent off to bed immediately after supper but they get up at half past eleven and prepare to put the escape plan into action. Huck has forgotten to obtain some butter; he goes down to the cellar for it and is caught by Aunt Sally as he emerges. She sends him into the sitting-room, where fifteen farmers have collected, with their guns. After Aunt Sally sends him back to bed, Huck slips outside to Jim's hut, where Tom is waiting for him, and warns his friends that the farmers are about to surround the hut. When the armed men do arrive, in the darkness and confusion the three of them manage to get as far as the fence. Tom makes a noise climbing over it and the farmers pursue them with dogs towards the river, letting off their guns (p. 348). The fugitives dodge off the track; the dogs, recognizing them, 'only just said howdy, and tore right ahead towards the shouting and clattering' (p. 348). Huck, Tom and Jim use Huck's canoe to paddle over to an island where the raft is moored. Tom is bleeding badly from a gun-shot in his leg and Jim refuses to cast off: he insists that they must fetch a doctor to look at Tom's injury. Tom reluctantly agrees, specifying that the doctor must be blindfolded on his way to the island. Huck sets off to bring a doctor from the town. It is agreed that Jim will hide while the doctor is on the island.

The most striking point in this chapter is Jim's generosity and sense of reality as he once more puts off his escape so that Tom's wound can be seen to. The reason he gives the boys is that if their positions were reversed, Tom Sawyer would have done the same for him (p. 349). What do *you* think? Huck approves of Jim's decision – but notice how he expresses himself: 'I knowed he was white inside' (p. 349). Huck has committed himself to Jim but he never completely throws off his racist upbringing. Note how p. 347 echoes one of the opening episodes of the book (p. 53). In both, the two boys and Jim are close enough to touch each other but unable to see in the dark. On this second occasion, they are united in purpose – Jim's escape. Perhaps this and other echoes may give us a clue to the intended effect of the closing chapters; but it is hard to believe in the way Huck and Jim so passively accept Tom's shallow fantasies after all they have been through together.

CHAPTER 41, pp. 351–8

Huck tells the doctor that he and his brother have been hunting on Spanish Island and that 'Sid' has accidentally shot himself in the leg.

The doctor is nervous about crossing to the island in Huck's canoe and insists that it will not take Huck's weight as well as his own. Huck goes to sleep on a lumber pile and, when he wakes up, wonders what he will do if the doctor finds Tom's leg difficult to 'fix'. He runs into Uncle Silas, who says that Aunt Sally has been 'mighty uneasy' at the boys' absence (p. 352). Huck pretends they have been with the farmers who were looking for Jim and says that 'Sid' is at the post-office, waiting for news. They go there and naturally do not find him. Mr Phelps insists that Huck should return home with him, to reassure Aunt Sally. At the farm a group of neighbours is discussing the strange events of the night and the objects found in Jim's hut. They agree that it must all have been done by 'sperits' (p. 355). After the visitors have gone, Huck tells Mrs Phelps the same story as he had told her husband, adding that both of them have been slightly hurt. By evening, 'Sid' (Tom Sawyer) has still not come home and after supper Mr Phelps goes to look for him in the town. Mrs Phelps comes to sit by Huck's bed and asks him to promise that he will not go out that night. Huck is very touched by her affection, and by her concern for Tom, and gives her his word that he will stay in his room. Twice he slides down the lightning-rod but, seeing Aunt Sally sitting 'by her candle in the window with her eyes towards the road and the tears in them' (p. 357-8), he goes back to bed, resolving that he 'wouldn't never do nothing to grieve her any more'. At dawn he sees Mrs Phelps, still at her post, sleeping by the burnt-out candle.

Huck, removed from Tom Sawyer's influence, regains his quick sensitivity to other people's distress. He is touched by Aunt Sally's anxiety and overcomes his own inclination to go back to the island and see what has happened there.

CHAPTER 42, pp. 359–67

Uncle Silas goes into town again, seeking news of Tom. He is so worried that he has forgotten to hand his wife a letter from her sister, which he had collected from the post-office the day before. Now he remembers and hands it over; but before Mrs Phelps can read it, a crowd of people appears at the farm. With them is the doctor, and Jim, and Tom Sawyer, who is delirious and being carried on a mattress. Huck hides the letter as Aunt Sally rushes over to kiss Tom. He goes out to see what is happening to Jim: 'some of them wanted to hang Jim, for an example to all the other niggers around there, so they wouldn't be trying to run away . . . and keeping a whole family scared most to death' (p. 360). Others point out that if they lynch Jim they will have to pay compensation to his owner, when he turns up. Jim is put back into the hut, with blows and curses; this time securely chained and guarded. Jim does not protest; and he does not tell his tormentors that he knows Huck. The doctor appears and advises the men to 'be no rougher on him than you're obleeged to' (p. 360). The doctor had found he needed assistance to cut out the bullet in Tom's leg; and Jim had crawled out of hiding to help him. The doctor had been afraid to leave the island 'because the nigger might get away' (p. 361), and had stayed there until he had been able to make a signal to some men who rowed by in a skiff. They had landed and tied Jim up while he was asleep. All the time they had been on the island, Jim had nursed Tom, 'a nigger like that is worth a thousand dollars – and kind treatment, too . . . He ain't no bad nigger, gentlemen' (p. 361), says the doctor. The farmers relent to the extent that they agree not to curse Jim any more – and then they lock him up. Huck decides he must put in a good word for Jim with Aunt Sally, when he has got past the tricky question of why he did not tell her that 'Sid' was so badly wounded. The next morning, Tom wakes out of his delirium and, thinking that Jim has made his excape, gleefully explains 'the way the whole thing was done' (p. 363). When informed that Jim is 'in that cabin again, on bread and water, and loaded down with chains, till he's claimed or sold' (p. 364), Tom is shocked into a sense of reality. He tells Huck and Aunt Sally that Miss Watson died two months previously. She set Jim free in her will because 'she was ashamed she ever was going to sell him down the river' (p. 365). Tom admits he devised the whole 'evasion' plan because he had 'wanted the *adventure* of it' (p. 365). At this precise moment, there is a surprise visitor – Tom's guardian, Aunt Polly, who is Mrs Phelps's 'Sis'. She stands 'looking across at Tom over her spectacles – kind of grinding him into the earth' (p. 365). Aunt Polly sorts out the mixed identities of the two boys. She explains that when she heard from Aunt Sally that 'Sid' had arrived, she had written for an explanation – but had

An Account of the Plot: **Chapter the Last (pp. 368–9)**

received none. (Tom had intercepted her letters and hidden them.) 'So now I got to go and trapse all the way down the river, eleven hundred mile, and find out what that creetur's up to, *this* time' (p. 366).

The farmers' handling of Jim is only a slightly milder version of crowd behaviour farther up river. The satire here is fairly good-humoured: Twain has already made his point and anything fiercer would disrupt the slightly cosy atmosphere of life at Phelps's farm. By the end of the chapter, there are only a few loose ends of the plot left to tie up.

CHAPTER THE LAST (pp. 368–9)

Huck wants to know what Tom had planned to do if they had got away on the raft with Jim. Tom says he had intended to go down to the mouth of the river. There he would have told Jim he was free and meant to bring him back home in style, on a steamboat, and 'waltz him into town with a torchlight procession and a brass band' (p. 368). The Phelpses are told how well Jim looked after Tom on the island. They release him and 'give him all he wanted to eat, and a good time, and nothing to do' (p. 368). Tom gives Jim forty dollars for taking part in the evasion plan. He wants all three of them to 'go for howling adventures amongst the Injuns, over in the Territory, for a couple of weeks or two' (p. 369). When Huck says he has no money 'to buy the outfit', he hears that his fortune is still safe with Judge Thatcher. Huck is afraid that Pap may turn up again to claim it; but Jim reassures him: the body in the frame house was Pap's (Chapter 9, p. 103). Huck decides that 'there ain't nothing more to write about'. The book ends on an open note, with Huck thinking that he may have 'to light out for the Territory ahead of the rest, because Aunt Sally she's going to adopt me and sivilize me and I can't stand it. I been there before' (p. 369).

So we are brought back to one main theme of the book – the clash between civilization and nature – by a reminder that Huck cannot settle down to a conventional life. But by the time we reach this 'happy ending', we have almost forgotten the clash in tone between the Phelps farm chapters and the great middle section of the book. Tom Sawyer has had his adventure and Jim does obtain his freedom. Huck's closing words raise a smile, but despite their neatness they cannot give a satisfactory end to his story because the conflict between the need for freedom and the need to find a place in society has not been resolved. Huck on his own is 'lonesome', yet he cannot settle down to the ordered life that society offers him. Mark Twain's message seems to be a bleak one: although society is corrupt, human beings cannot do without it entirely. Those who live outside it (Pap Finn) finally meet disaster and those inside must either prey on their fellow human beings or submit to convention. It is not surprising that Huck's future is left as a question mark.

Characters

HUCK

> *'A sound heart and a deformed conscience come into collision and conscience suffers a defeat'*
>
> MARK TWAIN

Huckleberry Finn, like Dickens's Scrooge and Mr Micawber, is one of those characters who have so caught popular imagination that they have burst out of their literary framework to lead an independent existence. Huck's true origin is the book that bears his name. He features in earlier and later writings by Mark Twain; but in *The Adventures of Tom Sawyer* he is only a sketch of his fully developed self; and, in the later books, as has been well said, we have another character masquerading under the name of Huck. His institutionalization as part of modern American folklore is a great irony in view of Huck's relationship with society.

The mainspring of Huck's actions is his longing to be free from social rules and conventions. This makes Huck accept his own kidnapping by Pap. Life in the log cabin by the river is easy-going and pleasant. But when Pap gets 'too handy with his hick'ry' (p. 75), Huck cuts free from him, too.

Life on the raft satisfies all Huck's needs: there are no social constraints; he has company; and there is the constantly changing riverside scene to engage his lively mind.

Despite a wish to be free, Huck is not a solitary by nature. The word 'lonesome' crops up frequently. Sometimes (pp. 51, 288), it denotes a mood of depression but most often it is used when Huck feels a need for human company. After 'hick'ry', Huck's main objection to life with Pap is that he is frequently left on his own for long periods. On Jackson's Island, after a day of blissful freedom, Huck again begins to feel 'lonesome' and is overjoyed when he finds Jim. In fact, Huck's ideal condition would be freedom without solitude – a dream that by the end of the book is shown to be impossible.

Huck's curiosity sparks off several episodes. On the very first page, he has rejected respectabilty and returned to his old rags and sugar-hogshead (p. 49). He is lured back to civilization by the promise of a place in Tom Sawyer's robber-band. Huck soon becomes bored with the imaginary adventures; but he is willing to hang on because he wants 'to see the camels and elephants' (p. 62). Even with Jim's company, Jackson's Island becomes 'slow and dull' and Huck longs 'to get a stirring up, some way' (p. 108). This is why he paddles ashore for his encounter with Judith Loftus. It is Huck's inquisitiveness – overruling Jim's common sense – that leads to the near-disastrous adventure on the *Walter Scott*.

Life has made Huck ruthlessly practical and any imagination he has is bent to that end. 'When I start in to steal a nigger, or a watermelon, or a Sunday-school book, I ain't no ways particular how it's done so it's done,' he tells Tom Sawyer (p. 319). He has a casual attitude to notions of personal property, helping himself to the produce of the fields as the raft floats by them. However, the widow's training has brought him to feel that what Pap calls 'borrowing' is a 'soft name for stealing' (p. 120); on Jim's suggestion they get it 'all settled satisfactory' by denying themselves two of the least desirable items. He is, however, completely free from the obsessive interest in money displayed by the other characters. His practical intelligence is not used for financial gain but only to keep himself (and later, Jim) out of trouble. This is shown by the ingenious plan to cover his tracks when he escapes from Pap's cabin and by the increasing fluency of his tall stories as he slips from one false identity to another.

Huck's common sense rarely deserts him – one notable exception being when he puts the dead snake on Jim's bed. Here he acknowledges the truth of someone else's beliefs because they have passed the test of practical experience – unlike the beliefs that Miss Watson and the Widow Douglas try to instil in him. The superstitions that form part of his background overlap those of black culture and in the novel are used to link human beings with nature. Huck's response to the

Mississippi and its natural surroundings provides the great poetic and lyrical passages in the book and shows Twain's most remarkable achievement in the use of dialect.

Huck is fatalistic; he 'wilts' before unpleasant experience but makes no long-term plans to fend it off. He deals with each situation as he encounters it. So long as his freedom is not impaired, he is eager to dip in and out of the social scene. He is friendly and adaptable. He accepts the king and duke on the raft without protest and accompanies them ashore, standing by to watch 'our gang' put on 'our' show. He fits in easily with the Grangerford and Wilks households but Huck does not take sides until circumstances put severe pressure on him to become actively involved. Normally, his attitude towards other people shows a mixture of warmth and detachment. Yet his sympathies are always touched by suffering or danger. The 'drunken' clown in the circus makes him ' all of a tremble' (p. 212); he tries, although unsuccessfully, to alert the watchman to the fate of the cutthroats on the steamboat. Huck is revolted by the results of the feud between the Grangerfords and Shepherdsons. He cannot bring himself to describe what happened when his friend Buck and another boy are killed trying to swim away down the river; he can feel compassion even for the two men who have wronged Jim and himself, those 'poor pitiful rascals' the king and the duke, when he sees them tarred and feathered: 'It seemed like I couldn't ever feel any hardness against them any more in the world' (p. 301).

It is the youthful resilience of Huck's nature that makes it possible for him to pass from one episode to the next, apparently without any emotional scarring. The horrifying incidents are shaken off, one after another, as a dog shakes off water, and Huck is still able to trust people, taking avoiding action only when it becomes necessary. His attitude towards ethics and morality would sound cynical in an adult: 'What's the use you learning to do right, when it's troublesome to do right and ain't no trouble to do wrong, and the wages is just the same? I was stuck . . . So I reckoned I wouldn't bother no more about it, but after this always do whichever come handiest at the time' (p. 149).

Is Huck a *developing* character? He increases in his ability to deal with the hazards of life along the river but what about his moral development and his relationships with people?

Huck has two dominant relationships in the book: one with Tom

Sawyer and the other with Jim. Huck sees through Tom's 'lies' but good-naturedly still falls in with his plans. He thinks of Tom many times during the voyage down the Mississippi; he measures his own success by what Tom would have done in his place. Huck's neutral attitude, in allowing Tom to put Jim through so many humiliating tricks before he can win his freedom, jars on many readers. There is an undeniable feeling that the relationship he has built up with Jim is being allowed to slide into the background. (See 'The Ending of *The Adventures of Huckleberry Finn*', p. 91.)

The pattern of Huck's deepening involvement with Jim is discussed in An Account of the Plot, in the notes on individual chapters. The key point is that though Huck comes to a heroic decision to 'go to hell' for Jim, he still thinks he is doing wrong. That is Twain's strongest hit against the Southern institution of slavery. It also means that Huck never comes to realize or think about his own beliefs.

In his mind, at least, Huck fights back against the religious beliefs of Widow Douglas and Miss Watson. He puts their theories to the test, so to speak, and they fail. He does the same with Tom's romantic fantasies; and he sees through the 'slush' talked by the king. If he fits in with any of this, it is not because he accepts that there is any truth in it – it is for the sake of social harmony or because he is 'lonesome' and wants company, or just because that is the way things are.

However, he is unable to disagree with the South's assumptions about slavery. In three episodes that show Huck's deepening affection for Jim, he wrenches himself away from his inbred Southern attitude to slavery – but he does it for purely personal reasons. Huck shows an increasing tendency to break out of his passive spectator's role in other ways as well: he decides to help the Wilks girls; he voluntarily returns to civilization to help free Jim; he tries to warn the king and duke about the punishment being prepared for them. Yet his basic attitude to black people remains unchanged – as Twain shows by many of Huck's remarks. Two striking examples are in his first conversation with Aunt Sally (p. 291), where his reply, when she asks him if the (imaginary) accident on the steamboat has hurt anyone, is, '"No'm. Killed a nigger"' and in the way Huck praises Jim for giving up his chance of freedom to help the doctor look after Tom: 'I knowed he was white inside' (p. 349).

JIM

Jim is a key figure in the plot of *The Adventures of Huckleberry Finn*, for it is his flight from Miss Watson that is the reason behind the voyage down the Mississippi. He is also there to provide the situations in which Huck's 'sound heart' will defeat his 'deformed conscience'.

Up to the moment when he is to be 'sold down the river', Jim has been docile and obedient, and shown no signs of resenting the right of 'white folks' to treat him as a piece of property. We are told, however, that 'Jim was most ruined, for a servant', because he received so much attention from other slaves after Tom played the trick on him described on p. 54.

Jim is illiterate (it was an offence to teach a black person to read or write); his world is confined to direct experience in his own area; he cannot even grasp the idea that another language exists (p. 135). Yet his first actions after leaving the widow's house show his intelligence and resourcefulness.

Jim takes a protective attitude to Huck almost from their first encounter on Jackson's Island. He insists that they should remove their stores to the dryness of the cave (p. 101); he prevents Huck from looking at his dead father because the boy may be upset by the 'gashly' face of the corpse (p. 103).

Jim's relief and joy when he is reunited with Huck after the fog (p. 140) makes Huck's mean trick seem even shabbier. When told that he has dreamt the whole incident, Jim sits in silence for five minutes 'studying over it'. His trust in Huck is so absolute that he takes his friend's word against the evidence of his own senses. His dignified rebuke gives Huck his first insight into Jim's right to be treated as a human being.

Jim's wife and children enter twice into the story, each time as part of an incident in which Huck's racist attitudes are put to the test. On the first occasion (p. 146), Huck is horrified to learn that Jim has already planned to be reunited with his family, even if it means – as a last resort – that he must get an 'Ab'litionist' to go and steal them. In the next incident (pp. 218–19), Jim talks about his remorse for having hit his daughter, when he thought – mistakenly – that she had disobeyed him. Huck is struck not by Jim's love for the little girl but by the startling possibility that 'he cared just as much for his people as white folks does for their'n'.

Jim grows in stature throughout the book. When he has been sold to the Phelpses by the king and duke, he generously gives up his chance to make a dash for freedom because the doctor needs someone to help him treat Tom Sawyer's wounded leg. He crawls out of hiding and so in effect gives himself up (p. 361).

It is the gradual revelation of Jim's fine and sensitive nature that makes the trivial comedy of the final chapters so offensive to many readers. However, it must be pointed out that once the raft overshoots Cairo, Jim makes no attempt to advance his own ideas on how the journey should proceed. He allows himself to be tied up for hours on end while the king and duke pursue their business ashore – and so does Huck. Jim makes only a couple of mild protests about the two frauds: 'I doan' mine one er two kings, but dat's enough' (p. 196) and 'dese kings o'ourn is reglar rapscallions' (p. 216). He manages to get himself transformed into a '*Sick Arab – but harmless when not out of his head*' (p. 220) but, essentially, he lets the 'white folks' dominate him in the middle section, as well as in the Phelps farm episode.

At the end of the book, Jim shows no resentment on hearing that he has been free for two months. He is 'pleased most to death' when Tom gives him forty dollars for being such a patient prisoner. The sum is significantly the same as the amount of money the king received for selling him to the Phelpses. This detail could be either a subtle comment on the fact that a black person cannot attain true freedom in a racist society or it could be merely another brushstroke in establishing Jim's forgiving, generous nature. Our decision about this must depend on how we view the last section of the book. (See 'The Ending of *The Adventures of Huckleberry Finn*', p. 91.)

TOM SAWYER

Tom Sawyer represents, in juvenile terms, the 'dreams and phantoms' which corrupt Southern society. He plays a much narrower role than in the book named after him: there, he is on the side of anarchy and freedom. In *The Adventures of Huckleberry Finn* the emphasis is on

Tom's obsession with romantic literature and the way he tries to bend reality to fit into this framework. Huck rejects Tom's genies and 'A–rabs' in disgust, bracketing them with the Sunday-school stories of Miss Watson.

Nevertheless, Tom's personal magnetism is so strong that he can impose his own views on his friends, who never question his right to take charge of any situation. Even Huck finds his hold unbreakable. Huck makes Tom's opinion his justification for boarding the *Walter Scott*. The highest praise Huck can give himself when helping the Wilks girls is, 'I reckoned Tom Sawyer couldn't a done it no neater himself' (p. 261). Tom's spirit hovers over the middle section of the novel; it is almost inevitable that he should reappear.

The first encounter of the two boys near Phelps's farm (p. 295) shows Tom momentarily losing his confidence, as he sees what he takes to be Huck's ghost. 'You come in here and feel of me if you don't believe me,' says Huck. (Whether conscious or unconscious, this is one of several scriptural parodies in the novel.) The doubting Thomas recovers quickly from his fright: 'he wanted to know all about it right off; because it was a grand adventure, and mysterious, and so it hit him where he lived' (p. 295).

The leader–follower relationship is quickly re-established between Tom and Huck, and from then on the voyage down the Mississippi is reduced to the status of a 'grand adventure'. There is a striking contrast between the devious, cautious way in which Huck has approached the riverbank communities and the confidence with which Tom walks into the Phelps house and plays his joke on Aunt Sally (p. 298). Tom has an assured place in society. Basically, he in conventional – as is shown in the meticulous way he makes Huck pay for the watermelon (p. 314) and himself lays five cents on the table when he takes some candles from Mrs Douglas's kitchen (p. 54).

Tom's apparent willingness to help free Jim is a great shock to Huck, who of course is not aware that Jim is free already. The cruelly selfish 'evasion' plans nearly end in tragedy, when Tom's romantic fantasies collide with the fear he has stirred up among the adults by his 'nonnamous' letters. There is a distinct parallel between Tom Sawyer and Buck Grangerford; the difference in their fates highlights the fact that here Mark Twain is using his material in a humorous way and not to make a savage attack on Southern society. (This variation in approach adds to the complexity of *The Adventures of Huckleberry Finn* and is one of the reasons why it is so difficult to decide what effect Twain was aiming at in these final chapters.)

When he is told that Jim is 'in that cabin again, on bread and water, and loaded down with chains, till he's claimed or sold!' (p. 364), Tom is jolted out of his dream-world and reveals that Jim is free. But he seems quite unaware that his pranks might have led to Jim being lynched and is unrepentant about all the trouble he has caused. It is sufficient excuse that he just 'wanted the *adventure* of it' (p. 365).

Tom's last appearance in the book is when he invites Huck and Jim to 'slide out of here' (p. 368) and 'go for howling adventures amongst the Injuns' (p. 369). Whether Tom will ever manage to get away from Aunt Polly and go to this 'haunt of criminals and fugitives' (Notes, p. 394), and whether his carefully sheltered fantasies would survive such an experience, is left an open question.

PAP FINN

Pap Finn, Huck's father, comes over as one of the most unpleasant characters in the book. His entry is built up to by the discovery of a drowned man in the river, who at first is thought to be Pap (p. 61); and then by Huck's panic-struck reaction when he sees his father's boot-tracks in a fresh fall of snow (p. 66). When he turns up in Huck's bedroom his sinister appearance justifies all Huck's dread of meeting him again: 'His hair was long and tangled and greasy, and hung down, and you could see his eyes shining through like he was behind vines ... his face ... was white; ... a tree-toad white, a fish-belly white' (p. 69).

Pap is a 'poor white', at the bottom of the ladder in Southern society – white society. He is bitterly resentful that his son has 'put on considerble many frills' since he last saw him. Huck is learning to read and write, has become a 'sweet-scented dandy' and sleeps in a proper bed, while Pap had 'to sleep with the hogs in the tanyard' (p. 70). (Twain seems to be writing a parody on the Return of the Prodigal Son.) Pap is afraid that Huck may even 'get religion' (p. 70). All this is very

Characters: Pap Finn

ironic, since, as we know, Huck finds these 'frills' of civilized life very hard to stomach.

As Huck had feared, Pap's main object is to get his hands on Huck's six thousand dollars. This sum has already been 'sold' to Judge Thatcher. Pap then turns his efforts to taking Huck away from Widow Douglas and Judge Thatcher, hoping that this will give him access to his son's fortune.

Pap is violent and a drunkard. He takes a grim pleasure in exploiting the gullibility of others if he has the chance, as when he is briefly taken into the household of the new judge (pp. 72–3). But most of the time his behaviour is quarrelsome and self-destructive. He is a social reject and appears only to make trouble.

When Pap takes Huck away to the log cabin, he treats him with great violence. His attitude is implicitly contrasted, later, with the care and affection shown to the boy by Jim. It is not surprising that Huck shows no trace of affection for his father and no regret when he learns of his death (p. 369).

In the argumentative stage of drunkenness, Pap 'cusses' the 'govment' (p. 77) that allows the law to separate a father and his child, Judge Thatcher, who is keeping him away from the six thousand dollars, and 'a considerable parcel of people which he didn't know the names of' (p. 76). His strongest 'cuss' is kept for the educated black man from Ohio, who offends Pap's precarious status as a member of white society on several counts: he is well-dressed, middle-class and is a 'p'fessor in a college' (p. 78). The crowning insult is that in his own state, as a free man, the Negro is entitled to vote. Pap refuses to share such a contaminated privilege – he has given up the right to use his own vote. Pap's only effective retaliation against the black man has been that he has 'shoved him out o' the way' (p. 78) – perhaps as an attempt at provocation, since Negroes could be beaten for hustling white people.

As Pap rants on to Huck, he passes into delirium tremens – a stage in alcoholic poisoning where the victim is overtaken by hallucinations. In a terrifying and ghastly scene he tries to kill Huck (p. 80). Although Pap appears to have recovered the next day, it is obvious that such episodes are going to occur more and more frequently. His sordid end, shot in the back in a gambling den, is not unexpected.

THE KING AND THE DUKE

These two confidence tricksters give rise to some of the funniest scenes in the novel. They are quite unscrupulous in the methods they use to prey on riverside society; but at least it must be said that they do not share its tendency to violence. They live off their wits, not their muscles. We cannot help feeling a sneaking admiration for the ingenuity with which they rise to every occasion, whether it be to 'make a fast buck' or to dodge out of trouble.

American humorists had already made great use of similar characters. One of them is the central figure in Herman Melville's *The Confidence Man* (1857), a satirical novel, which, like *The Adventures of Huckleberry Finn*, is set on the Mississippi.

We never learn the names of Twain's conmen; those they use to address each other – 'Bilgewater', 'Capet' – are comic variations on the lofty rank they claim. Their complete identification with their roles underlines the comparison between the two rogues and real kings and dukes: according to Twain, they behave in exactly the same way. The king and duke make a much more prolonged appearance in the novel than any other characters except Huck and Jim; through them, Twain brings into sharp focus his satire on certain aspects of Southern society. Just as aristocrats like the Grangerfords and the Shepherdsons are caught up in a false code of family honour, so the ordinary people of the area can be deceived by false piety and a hypocritical pretence of family affection.

Although the two tricksters show the same approach to life, Twain has managed to individualize them. The king is 'about seventy, or upwards' with 'a bald head and very gray whiskers' (p. 180). The duke is much younger, about thirty years old. The duke has his 'act' all worked out; he is the inspiration behind the theatrical performances and the Royal Nonesuch. He is also slightly less ruthless than the king; he devises the scheme of the 'Sick Arab' (p. 220), which allows Jim to remain unbound during the day; and he restrains the king when he begins assaulting Huck (p. 274). The king, however – no doubt because of his greater experience – is much quicker witted in exploiting whatever opportunity turns up. He cleverly outranks the duke with his claim to be 'the pore disappeared Dauphin' (p. 184);

and it is the king who masterminds the whole Wilks operation and whose nerve holds out longer, when the duke is afraid of being found out.

Through the Wilks episode, Twain shifts the readers' attitude towards the two rogues by emphasizing their absolute heartlessness. The Wilks sisters are sympathetic – if slightly sentimental – characters; they will be ruined by the conmen's greed. With the selling of the slaves, the king's and duke's behaviour is tied into one of the major themes of the novel – the attitude of Southerners towards black people. The incident prepares us for their final treachery when they sell Jim for 'forty dirty dollars'.

The last we see of the duke and the king is when they have suffered the fate that has threatened them all along – being tarred and feathered. It is a remarkable tribute to Huck's generous spirit that he tries to warn the two men. He is unsuccessful; but when he sees them suffering this barbaric punishment, 'astraddle of a rail' (p. 301), he feels sorry for the 'poor pitiful rascals'.

MINOR CHARACTERS

The Adventures of Huckleberry Finn contains a large gallery of minor figures with sharply defined personalities, even though they may appear for only a few pages.

The characters in St Petersburg – Widow Douglas, Miss Watson, Judge Thatcher – are dealt with fairly gently, as are their counterparts at Phelps's farm – Aunt Sally and Uncle Silas (and Aunt Polly). They are drawn from Twain's own family and other adults who lived in Hannibal, Missouri, where he spent his boyhood. Twain shows that they are as steeped in racist attitudes as the rest, but with the exception of Miss Watson (who makes a death-bed repentance) the main emphasis is on their fundamental human decency – at least, to each other. Their attitudes to black people are a product of their society, springing from an environment for which they cannot be held personally responsible. The widow is shown as being more thoughtful and kinder than her sister. Her influence on Huck comes out in his remark, 'I judged she would be proud of me' (p. 131), when he tries to save the cutthroats on the *Walter Scott*; and in his doubts about the rightness of 'borrowing' produce from the fields (p. 120). The same treatment is shown in the characterization of the Wilks sisters and of Aunt Sally, particularly in the rather sentimentalized scenes on pp. 357 and 358.

Other characters provide a general portrait of Southern society. It must be said that there are very few likeable people among them. The Grangerfords and Shepherdsons appear for the sole purpose of underlining the violence generated by false and outdated codes of honour. This side of Southern life was investigated by Twain when he revisited the Mississippi basin in 1882, while he was writing *The Adventures of Huckleberry Finn*. The shooting of Boggs is based on a case that came up before Twain's father in 1845 (see Notes, p. 390). The incident must have made a deep impression on Twain as a boy – it is the most brutal piece of violence in the book.

Apart from these individual characters, we have a brilliant collection of crowd scenes, all minutely detailed. Through the revival meeting in Chapter 20, the behaviour of the mourners in Chapter 25 and the outraged reactions of the audience conned by the Royal Nonesuch Chapter 23, we are given a vivid picture of pre-Civil-War life round the Mississippi.

Commentary

NARRATIVE STYLE

The advantage of having a story told by the main character is that we can become directly involved with someone who seems to be speaking directly to *us*. The story can be told in everyday speech. There is a drawback, of course. We cannot be told about the thoughts or feelings of the other characters. We have to work these out from their actions; or sometimes the narrator will make comments, when looking back on events a long time after they occurred. In *The Adventures of Huckleberry Finn* Mark Twain did not make use of this possibility but narrowed the viewpoint even further. Huck does not have any later perspective: he seems to be writing very shortly after his adventures have come to an end. In fact, he seldom makes the kind of remarks we expect from someone telling his or her story. Apart from a few phrases here and there, it is only at the novel's opening and in the final paragraphs that Huck steps out of the story like a traditional narrator.

However, this restriction heightens the impact of the novel. Twain's hero is a boy old enough to join in the social life of adults, who still has the curiosity and fresh eyes of a child. We receive a uniquely vivid impression of life round the Mississippi basin, made even more three-dimensional by the illusion of someone talking aloud. We live through his experiences with Huck. It is interesting to remember that the novel was originally written as a single unit – there were no chapter divisions until the publisher insisted that the text should be parcelled out in the conventional way.

Huck speaks to us in his native south-western vernacular. It gives way only once, in Colonel Sherburn's speech (pp. 209–10), but otherwise it encloses the whole novel in a vast range of moods – poetic description of nature, broad comedy, scenes of suspense and violence, and dialogue that bounces off the page.

FORM AND STRUCTURE

The structure of a novel often depends on the development of its plot. This is what we might expect in *The Adventures of Huckleberry Finn*, where events follow one another in strict time sequence. There are no flashbacks, except for the brief explanations that occur when one character wants to bring another up to date. To decide what the plot of a novel is, we have to start by looking at the story-line, to see why it takes the particular direction it does and why the author chooses certain episodes – that is, we are trying to discover the aim or intention of the story.

The Adventures of Huckleberry Finn has two goals: Huck wants to escape from civilization and the beatings of his drunken, violent father; the slave, Jim, wants to escape to the freedom of the Northern states. These two aims blend in their joint voyage down the Mississippi. But neither remains dominant and only Jim's definitely succeeds. Huck is pulled back to civilization at the Phelps farm, long before the book ends. His often-quoted remark, '. . . reckon I got to light out for the Territory' (p. 369), does not really balance the weight of the preceding eleven chapters, in which he has been in exactly the same kind of conventional environment that he escaped from at the beginning. Besides, the quotation is incomplete: it ends with the words 'ahead of the rest' – the rest referring to Jim and to Tom Sawyer, who suggests this new adventure in the first place. This means that Huck's further bid for freedom (if he ever makes it) is already endangered by the world of Tom Sawyer and his romantic fantasies.

The second aim of the plot – Jim's quest for freedom – begins to leak away quite early. Huck and Jim plan to abandon their raft at Cairo, where the Ohio joins the Mississippi, and take a steamboat to the North. They overshoot the town and decide to paddle back up to the river-junction. But their plan is thwarted when they lose the canoe (p. 151). They have to wait until they have found another canoe, since the raft cannot travel up river. Another canoe turns up on p. 180 – yet there is no suggestion now that Jim should make a break for it. The whole crucial question of his freedom is only resolved as a by-product of Tom Sawyer's 'evasion' adventure, when the truth comes out in the most casual way and it is revealed that Jim has been free for the past two months.

Commentary: Form and Structure

It seems, then, that we have to look at more than the plot to discover the structure or framework of *The Adventures of Huckleberry Finn*, and we find that this has several different aspects to it. It is more complex than would at first appear.

The central portion (Chapters 17–21) has something in common with the picaresque novel, a form that developed in Spain in the sixteenth century. In this, the hero moves from one adventure to the next, living by his wits and encountering a wide variety of social situations. He is often accompanied by a faithful companion and there is usually an element of satire. Although, strictly speaking, the picaresque hero must be a rogue, the term is often widened to cover any episodic novel which moves from one setting to another – and this obviously fits in with some aspects of *The Adventures of Huckleberry Finn*. However, in the opening chapters we are in the static, rather stifling society of St Petersburg and Huck returns to a very similar setting in Chapter 32 onwards, when he is reunited with Tom Sawyer at the Phelps farm.

This would seem to indicate a neat and deliberate pattern of three balanced divisions – a centre of movement and adventure, framed by two static sections. Even this explanation, however, is not satisfactory, as at a deeper level we find several structural elements both placed inside and crossing over these boundaries. By the end of Chapter 16 (the point where Twain abandoned the book in 1876), Huck has had to face up to his 'deformed conscience' in the first of three decisive rejections of Southern attitudes to slavery. Several other major themes have also been planted and Huck has already assumed several fictitious identities – a pattern that will follow him right up to the end of the book.

Nevertheless, the movement of the novel is circular: Huck ends up not just in a similar setting but one identical to the society he escaped from. He has been drawn back into the clutches of Tom Sawyer and he is about to be adopted once more by one of the female adult characters. There are striking parallels between the opening and closing chapters. Huck is shut up in a log cabin by Pap and has to make his escape; Jim is shut up during the 'evasion' plot. Tom Sawyer's romantic fantasies rule Huck at both the beginning and end of the novel.

We also find unmistakable echoes from one part of the book to another. A Romeo and Juliet situation accelerates the mutual slaughter of the Grangerfords and Shepherdsons: there is a farcical reminder of this as the king and duke rehearse the balcony scene from Shakespeare's play. Jim tells us about his little daughter's deafness and later the duke mimics a deaf-mute. Jim is sold to the Phelpses for 'forty dirty dollars' (p. 281) and later receives exactly the same sum from Tom Sawyer (p. 368) for being such a patient prisoner. These are only a few of the repetitions that link separate parts of the book together.

Another structural element is the rhythmic a.b.a.b. swing of episodes in Chapters 8 to 18, contrasting the dangers and corruption of the shore with the idyllic existence of Huck and Jim on the raft. Until the invasion of the king and duke (p. 180), the raft is the only place where honesty and freedom flourish.

We may also class as structural any feature that contributes to the unification of the novel, such as the single viewpoint, the strict chronological sequence and the use of dialect for both narrative and dialogue.

The main unifying factor is of course the Mississippi, the 'monstrous big river' that flows through the whole novel. Apart from its symbolic function (which we shall look at later) the Mississippi provides the background that links the separate episodes. Its varying moods and appearances have a major role to play in creating the atmosphere of many of the scenes in *The Adventures of Huckleberry Finn*. The Mississippi's function in the novel is to supply two sharply contrasted environments. Safe on their raft, Huck and Jim can live in harmony with nature. The river is indifferent to them, and sometimes dangerous, but it frees them from the shackles imposed by society. Huck's moments of remorse and tortured guilt arise only when society casts its shadow over his life on the raft.

The Mississippi is also a moving road, mobilizing a complex of trade and industry. It joins isolated communities, sending through them a stream of footloose, rootless people, like the king and the duke. Into a rural setting, it imports the seething restlessness of a large city, typical of America in the mid-1800s.

The overwhelming influence of the river is due to Twain's own involvement with it, both as a boy and as a steamboat pilot. By the time he wrote *The Adventures of Huckleberry Finn*, its importance as a highway had shrunk before the expanding railroads. Twain's nostalgic love for the river obviously remained constant – unlike his attitude to the communities on its banks. Their inhabitants are shown as being cruel, gullible, hypocritical and totally corrupted by the institution of slavery. They are satirized in episodes that have little to do with the main plot. Without them, however, the book would give a much less rich and detailed picture of life in the Mississippi basin; so we must say that the recurring satirical episodes are also a structural feature of *The Adventures of Huckleberry Finn*.

IMAGERY AND SYMBOLISM

Although so successful as a novelist himself, Mark Twain was not interested in the novel as a literary form. In one of his letters, he complains about not being able to read the works of three famous novelists on account of their 'tedious analyses of feelings and motives' and because he can understand 'what they are at a hundred years before they get to it'. After finishing *The Adventures of Huckleberry Finn*, Twain spent seven months revising it, but this for Twain meant 'talking and talking and *talking* until it sounds right' – that is, bringing it as close as possible to the spoken word. He did not work intensively on the overall shape of the book. Consequently, it is sometimes difficult to decide what elements were deliberately inserted by Mark Twain, as opposed to those rising unconsciously from his creative imagination. This can present a writer with images and symbols that stand for far more than their literal meaning. The two main symbols in *The Adventures of Huckleberry Finn* are the raft and the river.

Both represent freedom but in a slightly different way. Between his two attempts to write *The Adventures of Huckleberry Finn*, Twain produced *A Tramp Abroad*, a fictionalized account of travels in Europe. It contains the account of an imaginary voyage down the Neckar river by raft, in which Twain refers to the 'restful influence', the 'deep and tranquil ecstasy' to be found aboard a raft. In the same vein, Huck remarks that 'what you want, above all things, on a raft, is for everybody to be satisfied, and feel right and kind towards the others' (p. 185). On the raft, there is release from social conflict and inner tension. Huck's and Jim's friendship grows through their being direct and honest with each other; there is no need for the pretence and disguises that Huck adopts in order to function with the communities he finds ashore.

The river embodies the outer aspects of freedom – complete withdrawal from human society into the harmony of nature. It can also be seen as a symbol of human life – 'the river of life' is a well-known phrase – and the two friends journey down it, passing from one encounter to the next, as human beings pass through life, unable to turn back, being constantly faced with new and surprising circumstances. At a deeper level, the river can be taken as the creative energies of life itself, restoring and renewing the human soul every time there is a return to this non-rational source of existence. Each time he leaves the river for the shore, Huck takes on a new identity. Connected with this is a repeated cycle of death and rebirth. Huck fakes his own death when he flees to the river. We are reminded of this twice: by Jim's terror at meeting him on Jackson's Island (p. 94) and by the reaction of Tom Sawyer when Huck goes from the Phelps farm to meet him (p. 295). Both think that Huck is a ghost come to haunt them. Like the seventeen suits thrown off by the clown on horseback (p. 212), Huck's disguises are shed one after another until he is 'reborn' as Tom Sawyer: 'it was like being born again, I was so glad to find out who I was' (p. 293).

Much of the action of *The Adventures of Huckleberry Finn* occurs at night. If you make a list of the settings for different episodes, you will be surprised to find how few of them take place in daylight. Images of gloom and darkness run throughout the book. So also does the imagery associated with death. Apart from the actual deaths that occur during the story – Pap, the Grangerfords, old Boggs and the men on the *Walter Scott* – there is the whole method of Huck's escape from his father; the obsession of Miss Watson with life after death; Pap's hallucination in which he sees Huck as the Angel of Death; the steamboat search for Huck's body; the gruesome 'embalming' of Emmeline Grangerford's memory, and the whole background to the Wilks episode, which covers Chapters 24–30. Moreover, Huck's 'tall stories' are full of death and loss. Imagery such as this gives emphasis to the point of view that Twain is trying to put over. Behind the humour, and Huck's marvellously vivid dialect, Mark Twain is trying to draw our attention to aspects of Southern life which he considered would result in its destruction.

THEMES

Twain puts his views across by introducing into the book a number of themes, which are brought out by the way the material of the story is manipulated. We shall cover some of the most important here. They are: *Slavery and Freedom*; *Religion and Superstition*; *'Forty Dirty Dollars'*; *'Dreams and Phantoms'*.

Slavery and Freedom

Twain is concerned with freedom from two kinds of slavery: the 'slavery' of having to conform to the fixed rules of society, and institutionalized slavery, in which one set of human beings can have property rights over another. The two run parallel, as is shown by the journey that Huck and Jim make together. Neither kind of bondage is discussed in any abstract way; Mark Twain's opinions on them are demonstrated by the situations and events of the novel.

The slavery of society, as experienced by Huck, lies in the middle-class standards of behaviour imposed by Widow Douglas and Miss Watson. In the opening pages of *The Adventures of Huckleberry Finn*, these are presented humorously as the tiresome rules resented by every healthy child – tidiness, punctuality, regular meals and respect for adult authority and wisdom. (Jo, the tomboy heroine of *Little Women*, by Twain's contemporary, Louisa May Alcott, displays the same attitude as Huck.) However, this attack on a particular code of behaviour, that of small-town America, broadens out to a much wider theme: flight from the corrupting influence of civilization to the free and innocent world of nature. The idea is reinforced by the use of a child-narrator – childhood being accepted as the 'innocent' stage of life.

Rejection of society is found in the work of other nineteenth-century

American writers, notably Henry David Thoreau (1817–62) and James Fennimore Cooper (1789–1851). Fennimore Cooper's 'Leatherstocking Tales' features a hero who sets out to find adventure and his true identity in the wilderness. This tradition is still reflected in some Western films.

The reality of American frontier history ensured the popularity of such a subject for fiction; but as a literary idea it goes back to the European Romantic movement, generally considered to have begun with the French philosopher, Rousseau (1712–78). Later writers, such as the poet William Blake (1757–1827) and the Lake poet, William Wordsworth (1770–1850), not only regarded nature as the only true home for the human spirit, but also believed that childhood had an instinctive closeness to nature that was corrupted by the experience of living in society. 'Boy-life out on the Mississippi', the subject of *The Adventures of Huckleberry Finn*, has a clear connection with these ideas. The most poetic passages in the novel occur when Huck feels released from the tensions and pressures of society, and 'lazies along' in communion with the river.

The American Civil War (1861–5) was fought between North and South on the issue of Negro slavery; after it, all slaves were emancipated. So Twain's novel, published in 1884–5, might be seen as dealing with a cause already won. But black Americans, although technically free, continued to suffer many disadvantages, and the racist attitudes which had grown up round the institution of slavery were still very much alive. The Ku-Klux-Klan, associated with the intimidation and lynching of Negroes, was founded in 1868. (There is a reference to it in Colonel Sherburn's speech on p. 210) Although we learn a lot about the laws relating to Negroes in the 1840s, Twain was not trying to give a strict historical account. He wanted to show how deeply rooted racist views were in the minds of Southerners and how they corrupted the whole of society. Twain himself came from a slave-owning family. Looking back at his own slow and painful change of heart, he writes: 'the wise and the good and the holy were unanimous ... that slavery was right ... a condition that the slave himself ought to be thankful for'. (Thankful, that is, that the white owners looked after their slaves, just as a good farmer would be considerate towards his animals.) However kind the owners, the slaves were still regarded as disposable property.

Commentary: Themes

We see the results of this attitude at many different levels. Pap makes a vicious verbal attack on a man obviously much more intelligent and better-educated than himself, who 'wouldn't a give me the road if I hadn't shoved him out o' the way' (p. 78). '... why ain't this nigger put up at auction and sold?' is his immediate reaction at seeing this affront to his dignity as a white person. When Jim is recaptured and brought back to the Phelps farm, the only reward that his generous self-sacrifice receives is that the farmers promise 'that they wouldn't cuss him no more' (p. 362). In the case of the Wilks sisters, Twain demonstrated that genuine kindness can co-exist with racist attitudes by showing the girls' distress that their slaves are to leave them and also be parted from their families.

Racism infects the slaves themselves, so that they accept the idea of their own 'inferiority'. Asked what he would do if someone said to him '*Polly-voo-franzy*' (p. 135), Jim replies that he would 'bust him over de head. Dat is, if he warn't white. I wouldn't 'low no nigger to call me dat.' When the Grangerford slaves squabble over the raft, finding it after the disastrous collision with a steamboat, Jim recovers it with a veiled threat: 'I ast'm if dey gwyne to grab a young white genlman's propaty, en git a hid'n for it?' (p. 172).

The strongest attack on slavery is mounted through Huck's struggle with his 'deformed conscience'. His three major encounters with his own racism are discussed in the notes to Chapters 15, 16 and 31. But Huck never draws any general conclusions from these experiences that would change his perspective on the way that Negroes and 'white folks' should relate to each other. In coming to his great decision to 'go to hell' for Jim, Huck is not acting on principle. He does not *consciously* balance his affection for Jim against social duty and decide that the latter is false. His own view of the situation is that he cannot bear the shame of betraying Jim's generosity. Jim has 'petted' him, doing Huck's watch-duty as well as his own, trusted him even at times when Huck has thought of giving him up, and shown overwhelming joy when they were reunited after the separations caused by the fog and the collision with the steamboat. Huck still thinks he is doing wrong in sticking to Jim. In his own mind, he never completely breaks down the barriers between black and white.

It is hard to tell how far these reservations were deliberately written into the book. Twain states emphatically elsewhere that slavery is a 'bald, grotesque and unwarrantable usurpation' (of human rights), yet he patronizingly describes Uncle Dan'l (the original of Jim) as someone 'whose head was the best one in the Negro quarter'. Black writers and critics have labelled Jim 'a white man's inadequate portrait of a slave'. One modern publisher removed the offensive word 'nigger' entirely from his edition of *The Adventures of Huckleberry Finn*. Do you agree with this? (At the time of writing, 'nigger' was a synonym for 'Negro slave' and not a term of abuse in itself.)

Religion and Superstition

Mark Twain passionately believed that no society could sincerely profess Christian values if it approved of slavery. Some of his most ferocious satire is directed against organized religion. In the novel, Huck himself appears merely puzzled by the trappings of religious belief. His practical mind cannot take in the mythology of heaven and hell. His disgust at what he called 'soul-butter and hogwash' is turned against the obvious insincerity of the king and duke. Huck is not hostile to religion as such – he merely finds it irrelevant.

This viewpoint gives Twain the chance to write some explosive criticism of so-called 'Christians' into the novel. The best example is the way the Grangerfords and Shepherdsons attend the same church, armed with their guns, shortly before they slaughter each other (p. 169). It is underlined that this is no mere ritual, carried out for the look of it. They are keenly involved in the service: 'everybody said it was a good sermon, and they all talked it over going home, and had . . . a powerful lot to say about faith, and good works, and free grace' (p. 169).

A less savage attack appears in Chapter 20, where the king poses as a reformed pirate and makes a handsome profit from the collection taken to reward his return to righteousness. Twain is laughing at the gullibility of people so eager for emotional excitement that they are easily deceived. We see the same effect round Peter Wilks's coffin, where the king works the mourners up to such a pitch that 'everybody . . . busted out and went off sobbing and swabbing' (p. 228); and a sly dig at the shallowness of such feelings when a dog barking in the cellar rouses such curiosity in the mourners that the undertaker has to investigate and return with the news that '*He had a rat!*'. After which, everyone can turn their minds back to the funeral! (pp. 246–7).

These scenes are set pieces, full of broad comedy. The behaviour of individuals is criticized at a more sophisticated level. Miss Watson and her sister, Widow Douglas, are full of conventional piety. Grace is said at meals and there are prayers for the whole household at night. Miss Watson tries hard to fill Huck with her own ambition 'to live so as to go to the good place' (p. 51). Yet Miss Watson cannot resist the lure of making a profit of eight hundred dollars by selling Jim. She knows she is doing wrong and is 'ashamed' at the end (p. 365) when she rather improbably dies and sets Jim free in her will – to make it up to him.

Similarly, at the Phelps farm, Uncle Silas is a lay-preacher with 'a little one-horse log church down back of the plantation, which he built . . . himself, at his own expense' (p. 297). He and Aunt Sally visit Jim in his prison and seem to feed him well. He is, after all, someone else's 'baptized property', as the phrase went in the South. Yet for all their kindness, Jim is kept locked up for more than three weeks; when he escapes the Phelpses think it quite natural to organize a band of armed farmers to track him down with dogs.

Against the hypocrisy and contradictions of organized religion, Twain sets the world of superstition and magic, with its hold on people's basic fears. Some of the folklore overlaps the world of the 'white folks'; most of it, however, belongs to Negro culture. Rationally, we know that Nat's and Jim's superstitions are unfounded; but by associating them with the river and the natural world, Twain invests them with a dark and primitive power.

'Forty Dirty Dollars'

Most of the characters in *The Adventures of Huckleberry Finn* are activated by desire for money and justify their actions by translating them into cash values. The opening adventure has Tom Sawyer stealing candles from the kitchen and leaving five cents in payment (p. 54);

at the end of the book he pays Jim forty dollars for taking part in the 'evasion plot' – an echo of 'forty dirty dollars' (p. 281) and of the sum with which the slave-hunters salve their consciences for not helping what appears to be a family gone down with smallpox (pp. 148–9). Miss Watson, of course, justifies betraying her promise to Jim because 'sich a big stack o' money she couldn' resis'' (p. 96).

Greed for money is responsible for several of the disasters in the book. The two cutthroats on the *Walter Scott* drown with their victim because they go back to collect his share of the loot, and so allow Huck and Jim to escape by using their skiff (p. 127); the watchman on the ferry-boat is reluctant to set out to rescue them, until he is sure he will be paid for his trouble – and by then it is too late (pp. 130–31). When the king and duke are exploiting the Wilks sisters, it is because the king insists that they stay on to collect every cent of profit that they are found out.

In strong contrast, Huck at the beginning of the book is anxious to get rid of his fortune of six thousand dollars – the discovery of his son's sudden wealth being the only reason, of course, that Pap wants to renew contact with Huck.

'Dreams and Phantoms'

One central theme in *The Adventures of Huckleberry Finn* is the difference between appearance and reality, brilliantly caught in the image of the 'drunken' clown who is finally revealed as 'slim and handsome, and dressed the gaudiest and prettiest you ever saw' (p. 212). The tricks of the king and duke are practised on people who do not see the gap between what they think they are and what they really are. They are an easy prey to conmen who use the pious, high-flying words they are used to, as at the revival meeting in Chapter 20 and in the hilarious scenes when the two rogues pretend to be Peter Wilks's brothers.

Huck's honest responses and his sharp eye repeatedly puncture the falsity of Southern life, even when he does not fully understand what he describes. Twain shows this falsity operating at every level of society. He saw it as stemming from the distortions of a slave-based economy and the way the aristocratic plantation-owners clung to

Commentary: Themes

'dreams and phantoms, with decayed and swinish forms of religion, with decayed and degraded systems of government, ... sham grandeurs ... and sham chivalries ... of a ... worthless long-vanished society'. (That is, an outdated, mediaeval code of honour.) All this, according to Twain, was the fault of Sir Walter Scott and his romantic picture of feudal European society: 'It was Sir Walter who made every gentleman in the South a major or a colonel, or a general or a judge, before the war ... he who created rank and caste down here ... Sir Walter had so large a hand in making Southern character ... that he is in great measure responsible for the war.'

Before dismissing this as mere exaggeration, we should remember that the cotton farming which produced the Old South did not get properly into its stride until after the Napoleonic Wars (1815 onwards); the rapid change from small farmer to wealthy plantation-owner, for families like the Grangerfords, happened at the same time as a mania in the Southern states for Scott's Waverley novels and plays made from them. Plantations were named after the novels; mock tournaments were popular. (And later, the Ku-Klux-Klan summoned its members with the Highland fiery cross, found in the pages of Scott.)

Whatever their origin, these 'sham chivalries' are clearly at work in the feud between the Grangerfords and Shepherdsons, with its dreadful outcome. After the first piece of violence Huck witnesses, Mr Grangerford rebukes his son – not for taking an unjustified shot at Harney Shepherdson, but for doing it from behind cover, thus not giving Harney a sporting chance to kill him.

The adult code of honour is reflected in the rules of the games that Tom Sawyer imposes on his gang. Most are drawn from incidents in historical novels – a category of fiction that hardly existed before Scott. In the juvenile world the sham results in farce, not tragedy. Tom's friends have to deny the evidence of their eyes: a Sunday-school picnic becomes a caravan train of 'Spaniards and A–rabs'; a pick-axe must be called a case-knife, to hold up the illusion of romantic adventure. Huck sees through all this, but lets himself fall in with Tom's wishes, impressed, as he says, with his 'style'. At the ending of the book Tom's attempts to bring the adult world to share his fantasies provoke real danger and he is wounded by a real bullet.

The fate of the steamboat, *Walter Scott*, neatly sums up Twain's attitude to the delusions of romance and chivalry.

AMERICAN HUMOUR

By the time that Mark Twain embarked on his writing career, there was already a well-established tradition of American humour, usually based on life at the frontier. Two popular authors were Artemus Ward (1834–67) and Petroleum Nasby (1833–88). (These are both pen-names.) Ward posed as a travelling showman of waxworks and tame animals, deliberately using incorrect spelling and grammar for comic effect. Nasby brought ridicule on the upholders of slavery during the Civil War by writing illiterate letters to newspapers, in which he pretended to champion the South.

Twain defined American humour in this way: 'The humorous story is told gravely; the teller does his best to conceal the fact that he even dimly suspects that there is anything funny about it ... To string incongruities and absurdities together ... and seem innocently unaware that they are absurdities, is the basis of American art.'

This was the technique used by Mark Twain in his public lectures and readings – and, indeed, 'Mark Twain' was a carefully crafted personality, an apparently naive observer, in such books as *The Innocents Abroad*.

The Adventures of Huckleberry Finn has the same approach. Huck is literal-minded; he takes everything at face value. This gives rise to the humour in such episodes as the attempts of Miss Watson and her sister to teach Huck the difference between the 'good place' and the 'bad place', or in Huck's objections to their ban on smoking. In other incidents, Huck's straight-faced account tells more than he intends or understands: for instance, 'The judge he felt kind of sore' (p. 73) – his comment on this character's exasperation when Pap takes to the bottle again – shows up the judge's false claims to Christian charity.

To East Coast audiences, Mark Twain was primarily an exponent of frontier humour. Among its other characteristics – all to be found in Twain's works – were exaggeration, tall stories, low comedy, the verbal fun of puns, misspellings, lively vernacular dialogue, and the rather more sophisticated forms of burlesque and parody (that is, making fun of literary forms by using them in a ridiculous way), together with garbled history.

Many of these elements can be found in *The Adventures of Huckle-*

berry Finn. The 'tall story' appears in the succession of false identities produced by Huck for his visits ashore, as well as in its more usual form – the awful fate of Hank Bunker (p. 108) and Jim's account of the witches (p. 54). The whole sequence involving the king and duke is full of many types of frontier humour.

Burlesque, parody and garbled history ('Ode to Stephen Dowling Bots, Dec'd', pp. 161–2; the Shakespeare muddle, pp. 198–9, and Huck's history lesson on p. 217) all depend on a fair degree of cultural knowledge in the reader for the point to be grasped. So does the satire on romantic fiction in the Phelps farm section, when Tom Sawyer elaborates his plans to set Jim free. Here Twain is rather over-straining his use of Huck as narrator, even though the results are undeniably funny.

Ward and Nasby exploited the potential humour of bad spelling with forms such as *pollytiks* (politics), *sitterzens* (citizens), etc. You will find very few examples of this in *The Adventures of Huckleberry Finn*. Possibly Twain deliberately chose not to, thinking it might detract from the illusion of the speaking voice, or perhaps because it would have been difficult to combine this with the use of dialect for the serious passages in the book.

Another difference between Twain and earlier humorists is, of course, that his comic set pieces are not there merely to provide amusement. They interlock with other passages where a shift in tone or perspective changes farce to tragedy, in a bitter attack on Southern life. In the two chapters about the Grangerfords we are at first amused by Huck's naive descriptions of the family and by his conversation with Buck about the feud. But the ghastly outcome of this section and of others which also begin comically (think of the fate of the king and duke) take us far beyond the range of 'humour'.

LANGUAGE

Twain's great achievement in *The Adventures of Huckleberry Finn* was to extend the scope of vernacular writing. Using the phrases and rhythms of regional dialect he produced effects previously thought attainable only in 'literary' English. This was tremendously important in the development of American writing. In the context of *The Adventures of Huckleberry Finn* itself, the effect of using vernacular throughout is to remove barriers between the reader and the authentic voice of Huck. Almost every page of the book reflects his unique personality. Even when Huck merely stands by and reports on events, his comments as narrator bind him and us into the action.

The liveliness of the novel springs from its dialogue as well. Many of the conversations take place when Huck approaches strangers with some tall story to account for his presence. Apart from spinning his yarn, Huck is cautious and uncommunicative. He lets the other person chatter away – see, for instance, the garrulous Judith Loftus (pp. 110–16) and Aunt Sally (pp. 290–92).

Twain's 'Explanatory' (p. 48) claims that he used seven different south-western dialects. Critics agree that on the whole this is correct; although the variations are used more to distinguish individual speakers than to be minutely accurate. One of the most brilliant effects comes near the end of the book. After Jim's escape, the Phelps house is 'plumb full of farmers and farmers' wives, to dinner' (p. 353). They are discussing the extraordinary state of affairs in Jim's hut. They interrupt each other, break off for requests such as 'pass that-air sasser o' m'lasses, won't ye?' (p. 354), and chatter excitedly in broken sentences that vividly reproduce the babble of voices, yet at the same time individualize the speakers – especially old Mrs Hotchkiss, who bears everyone else down.

Besides using different dialect forms, Twain sharply contrasts the type of language used by his characters. To give only a few examples: Colonel Sherburn addresses the crowd (pp. 209–10) in scornful phrases that underline his cruelty and arrogance. His contempt here is well contrasted with the almost silent brutality with which he shot down the helpless old Boggs (p. 205). When they set out to gull their victims, the king and duke use a flashy style of rhetoric. Compare this with their sharp exchanges after the Wilks episode, when one conman is pitted against another (pp. 274–7).

In the narrative, several words and phrases appear again and again. *Monstrous*, *comfortable*, *lonesome*, *by and by*, *pretty soon* – all these help to maintain the themes of the book or make the narrative flow along. Twain also shows an almost Shakespearian inventiveness in finding new functions for words: '... the young man hove a sigh and says –

"Alas!" "What're you alassin' about?" says the baldhead' (p. 182). When the duke's bid for greatness is matched by the announcement that the 'baldhead' is the rightful king of France, Jim and Huck, to keep the peace, 'set to majestying him' (p. 185).

Such inventions also crop up in the most lyrical passages of the book. Poetic qualities are conveyed in a colloquial and apparently simple style that conceals very careful writing. Look for instance at the description of the storm on pp. 101–2. Huck's perceptions are vitally alive to its impact. The rain-drops 'thrash along'; the thunder goes 'rumbling, grumbling, tumbling'; the sky has 'darkened up'; the trees are 'dim and spider-webby'. (The last two phrases expand the usual way of using these words.) Contrast this with the slow, rhythmic descriptions of the river as Jim and Huck 'lazy along'. One of the finest is to be found in the opening pages of Chapter 19 (p. 177 onwards), but there are many others throughout the book. For many readers these evocations of the river in its different moods are the most memorable sections of *The Adventures of Huckleberry Finn*.

THE ENDING OF *THE ADVENTURES OF HUCKLEBERRY FINN*

As well as supplying the best-known quotation about *The Adventures of Huckleberry Finn*, Ernest Hemingway was also one of the first critics to express deep dissatisfaction with the last section of the book. Dating from a few years after he did this, there has been a great deal of discussion about the novel's 'problem' ending.

This is seen as the abrupt change of tone once Huck has been received into the household at the Phelps farm. Many readers feel that the whole significance of his voyage down the Mississippi with Jim is wiped out. After rejecting Tom Sawyer's fantasies at the end of Chapter 3, Huck falls under his spell again and lets Tom subject Jim to a series of humiliating incidents. Jim appears to revert to the stereotyped figure of the comic Negro. There are other complaints about the coincidences that round off the story, but the main attack is directed at the way the novel apparently loses the serious moral purpose of its middle chapters and trivializes its two main characters. It is probably not a coincidence that this uneasiness at the novel's ending came to the forefront during the rise of the black rights movement in America.

The discussion about the ending has followed four lines of thought which we will label A, B, C and D. You will have to decide for yourself which of them you find most convincing.

A. The distinguished poet and critic, T. S. Eliot, thought that it was right 'that the mood of the book should bring us back to that of the beginning ... For Huckleberry Finn, neither a tragic nor a happy ending would have been suitable ... Huck Finn must come from nowhere and be bound for nowhere.'

It must be said that most modern critics think that this view pays too much attention to the *form* of the book.

B. The second attitude is taken up by those who think that Mark Twain was a careless writer who wasn't aware of the greatness he had achieved in the middle chapters and reverted to a tiresome 'folksy' humour at the end.

C. This group of critics think that Mark Twain had definite aims and intentions in Chapter 32 onwards, but that the situation he had set up could not be resolved. The main points that come up, and the suggestions about them, are as follows:

The collapse of Jim into the 'comic Negro' figure

It is argued that Twain had pushed the relationship between a black man and a white boy as far as was plausible for the 1840s and acceptable to his readers. Jim's main role in this plot is to make Huck face up to the conflict between his heart and his conscience. Once Huck has torn up the letter to Miss Watson, Jim has no further part to play in the story.

The fact that Huck abets and aids a runaway slave implies serious legal and social consequences. Twain had to find a way to pull his hero out of that situation. He does it by the discovery that Jim has been already set free.

Miss Watson's melodramatic death-bed repentance seems very improbable. (So does her death.) Perhaps Twain was pointing in a direction which finally he could not bring himself to take – and which would have been unrealistic, given the attitudes of the people he was writing about: that is, a genuine change of heart on the part of a typical Southerner. The same could be said of Tom Sawyer, who plays a stupid trick on Jim in the opening pages of the novel and then at the end decides to help Huck set him free. Twain was unable to follow these ideas through and so we have Jim emancipated in a way that disastrously undermines the meaning of the voyage down the Mississippi.

It is pointed out that the lengthy 'evasion' chapters round off Twain's satire on 'sham grandeurs' and the pernicious influence of romantic literature. A black slave is substituted for the usual nobly born hero.

Huck's return to society

The novel had to end before the raft was swept out into the Gulf of Mexico. If we consider the whole direction of the novel – a voyage that goes deeper and deeper into slave territory, the innocence and good nature of Jim and Huck contrasted with the vicious societies of the river bank – then an unhappy ending seems inevitable. Hemingway suggested that the book should have ended with Jim being recaptured. In the tradition in which Twain was writing, an unhappy ending was unthinkable. Besides, the personality of Huck – optimistic and constantly shaking off the effects of his horrifying experiences – is against that. Yet Huck cannot be left on his own, in solitude. And if he returns to society, the St Petersburg or Phelps farm variety is the only kind he can be brought back to.

Finally, the argument runs, the ending is left open. There is no certainty that Huck will stay with Aunt Polly, any more than he did with the Widow Douglas.

D. There is a fourth school of thought that believes Mark Twain not only knew exactly what he was trying to do in the final chapters but also succeeded in his aim. Twain's intention, it is believed, is savagely ironic and far closer to the pessimism of his later writings than realized.

The freedom achieved by Huck and Jim on the river can only be an ecstatic dream, unless they cut themselves off from society completely and live in solitude. This is not acceptable to either of them: Huck gets lonesome; Jim yearns for his family and it is only by bargaining with society in some way that he can be reunited with them. Both Jim and Huck are bought back into society, without fully grasping its corruption. Jim is 'pleased most to death' with his forty dollars. Huck has two choices – either to degenerate into another version of Pap or submit to the cosy domestic values of small-town society. He will keep running away and keep returning.

The journey down the river *is* futile – that is why the book returns to farce at the end. The vision of the river is 'real' in one sense but so is society, with all its false values. Huck will never be able to maintain his freedom; and in a racist society it is impossible for a black man to keep his dignity. Jim is free only in the technical sense that he is no longer a slave.

This view takes a deeply pessimistic line on the possibility of human beings ever achieving happiness. Whether we accept it as a true interpretation of the ending of the novel depends on our response to the book as a whole. However, the fact that these final chapters have given rise to so much controversy and discussion – whatever opinion we have about them – must indicate that there is some flaw in Twain's masterpiece.

Glossary

Dialect forms of standard English words are not included; nor are Americanisms or phrases which can be understood from their context. In Jim's dialect, *th* at the beginning of a word, or in the middle, becomes *d*; the last letter – especially if it is *t*, *d* or *r* – is often dropped. For example: dat = that; de = the; jis' b'fo = just before; ole = old. Read any difficult sentences aloud and the meaning will usually become clear.

Ab'litionist: someone prepared to use illegal means to effect the abolition of slavery
allow: plan, decide, think
allycumpain: ointment to soothe insect bites
ambuscade: ambush
ash-hopper: equipment for sifting ashes

balditude: baldness
beatenest: strangest
beaver: type of hat
big-bug: important person
blame, blamed: damn, damned
blatter: talk vigorously
blethers out: shouts out
blimblammin': noise
blinders: leather blinkers or eye-flaps to stop a horse looking sideways
blossom: lovely character (sarcastic)

blow on: betray
bluff: steep
boss dodge: splendid trick
bottoms: low-lying land by river
brash: happy, confident
brisken up: decorate
bub: term of endearment
buck: male Negro
buckskin: soft, thin leather
bulge: advantage over; event (p. 342)
bull along: persist, continue
bullinesses: good ideas
bully: good, excellent
bullyrag: bully
busted: ruined, destroyed

camelopard: giraffe
camp-meeting: series of religious meetings held in secluded place

carpet-bag: travelling bag made of carpeting
case-knife: sheath-knife
cat-convention: noisy gathering of cats
cat-fish: very large fish – not the aquarium variety!
chance of: lot of
chaw: chew, bite-sized piece
chimbly-guy: supports steamboat's chimney
chippered: freshened up
chops: lips
cipher out: work out, figure out
clapboards: boards used to roof a cabin
closet: small room
colicky: sickly
comb up: smarten up
congress water: kind of mineral water
corn-cob: woody central part of an ear of maize
corn-crib: rack for storing corn-ears (maize)
cottonwood: American poplar
counterpin: bed covering
cowhide: beat
cravat (p. 275)*:* hangman's noose
crossing: where steamboat route has to cross from one side of river to other
cubby: very small room
currycomb: used for grooming horses

dead water: still, not moving in current
deadbeats: worthless people
deffisit: (deficit) shortage
dipper: long-handled container
dissentering: belonging to a non-established Christian sect, such as Methodist
dog-fennel: a variety of camomile
dog-leg: cheap tobacco
down the banks: reprimand
doxologer: a kind of hymn
draw a bead: take aim
drop onto: begin to think about
drug store: chemist's shop
duds: clothes

encores: extra items added to performance in response to applause

five-cent pieces: small coins
flapdoodle: false, inflated language
flapper: hand
fox-fire: glow from decaying wood
frame house: made of timber boards, not logs
frivolishness: frivolity

galluses: trouser braces
gap: yawn
gaudy: splendid, marvellous
genies: spirits
gingham: striped or checked cotton
goggles: spectacles
gourd: flask
greenhand: novice, beginner
guys: support ropes

haggled: cut
hair trunk: made of hide with the hair left on
hair-ball: formed by animal licking its fur or hair
hard lot: anti-social, not respectable
harelip: with the upper lip split
hark from the tomb: telling off
harrow: a spiked piece of farm machinery
heptarchies: seven early kingdoms
hick'ry: hickory stick
histrionic muse: goddess of drama and theatre
hive: save; hit
hived: robbed
hocus: deceive
hog: pig
hog drover: pig-herd or drover
hog-wash: nonsense, inflated language
hogged: acquired
hogshead: large barrel

holt (p. 182): act, trick
hook: borrow
hove at: direct at
howdy: hullo, how are you?
howdy do: fuss, commotion
hump: hurry
hunch: nudge
husky: strong powerful person

ingot: precious metal cast in a bar-shaped mould
inning: turn

jack-staff: flag-pole
jackass: donkey
jaks: country bumpkin
janders: jaundice, a disease
jimcracks: knick-knacks, ornaments
jimpson: thorn-apple
jug: drink (of alcohol)

lath: thin strip of wood
lay for: wait for
let on: pretend
level: sensible, intelligent
light, lit out: set out for
lightning-bug: firefly
limber: supple, flexible
limbs: (of tree) branches
linsey-woolsey: wool mixed with cotton or linen
looard: leeward, down wind – to lessen risk of infection
lumber: timber, wood
lynch: hang without trial

match half dollars: toss coins for winner
meeky along: go quietly
mesmerism: early name for hypnotism
mosey: go in leisurely way
mulatter: mulatto, child of one black and one white parent

nabob: important person
nigger-head: strong, dark tobacco of inferior quality

no slouch of, at: not easy, not insignificant
nonnamous: anonymous, not signed by writer
nuts for: very acceptable to, liked by

old pie: very friendly, pleasant
one-horse: small, insignificant
orgies: for 'obsequies', funeral ceremonies
ornery: inferior (much stronger than English 'ordinary')

palavering: idle chattering
pallet: straw mattress
pan out: work out
peart: confident, 'cocky'
peeled: bald
penitentiary: place for reforming criminals
persimmons: type of fruit
phrenology: the 'science' of deducing mental abilities from bumps on skull
planted: buried
play hooky: play truant
plug: compressed cake of tobacco
plumb: very, absolutely
pluribus unum: Latin phrase, used nonsensically here
poked: rowed
polly-voo-franzy: *parlez-vous-français?* Do you speak French?
pommel: front of saddle
pow-wow (verb): discuss secretly
pow-wow (noun): talking, noise; fuss (p. 196)
powderhorn: receptacle for gunpowder
preforeordestination: muddling of *predestination* and *foreordination*, two religious beliefs
primer: primary

quicksilver: mercury

rackety: noisy

ramrod: used to pack shot down barrel of gun
rapscallions: rascals
raspy: irritating
ratty: worn
reticule: small purse or bag
rip, rip out: bellow, utter violently
roust: awaken
rummies: drunkards
runaway prentice: an apprentice who does not stay to serve out his full time
rusty: having a 'hangover'

saddle boils: caused by friction between skin and saddle
saddle-bagged: grounded
sand: courage, 'grit'
sass: mock
seegars: cigars
set back: taken aback
seven-up: card game
shackly: broken down, ramshackle
shin: hurry
shot tower: used to make shot pellets by dropping molten lead into water from a height
show: chance, opportunity
sis: sister
skaddle: run away
skreeky: noisy
sloppy: wet
smack: kiss
smouch: steal
snag: obstacle, such as projecting stump of tree, etc.
soldier-plumes: plumes or feathers on helmet
soothering: calming
sot: stupid
soul-butter: false sentiment
spoon vittles: food that can be taken with a spoon only
squah (square): even, equal
sqush: collapse
starchy: 'posh'

startlish: surprised
store clothes: bought, opposed to home-made
stretcher: lie, exaggeration
study over: think over
sumter mules: pack animals
swab: wipe away (tears or sweat)
swap knives: make introductions

tanyard: place for curing hides
tar and feather: pour tar over, and then cover with feathers
teams (p. 192)*:* horses
temperance revival: campaign to persuade people to give up alcohol
togs: clothes
tote: carry
tow-head: see p. 118 of text
tract: religious pamphlet
traps: possessions, belongings
trapse: make one's way with difficulty or wearily
trash: rubbish; worthless person
trod the boards: acted on stage
tuck: spirit, courage
tuckered out: tired out
turn state's evidence: give evidence in return for pardon
turns himself loose: lets himself go

unities: rules of classical drama
up a stump: in difficulties
up to the hub: eager, ready
using: loitering

valley: valet, personal man-servant

wadding: used to pack bullets into guns before invention of cartridges
whale: beat
white caps: foamy top of waves
whoop-jamboreehoo: cry of alarm
wood rank: stack of timber

yaller-boys: gold coins
yaller-fever: tropical disease
yawl: small ship's boat

Discussion Topics and Examination Questions

DISCUSSION TOPICS

1. There is no direct criticism of slavery in *The Adventures of Huckleberry Finn*. How does the author make his attitude clear to us?

2. What do you feel about Tom Sawyer and why do you think he had such a strong hold over Huck?

3. Do you find the way that Jim wins his freedom satisfactory or would you have preferred a different ending to the book?

4. Can you sympathize with Huck's longing to get away from the people who want to 'sivilize' him?

5. What aspects of life in the Mississippi basin does Twain seem to be attacking (apart from slavery), and how does he do it?

6. 'The best way to get along with his kind of people is to let them have their own way' (p. 186). Is Huck too tolerant of the king and duke?

7. Leaving out Huck himself, which character in the book do you a. like most or find most interesting and b. dislike most? Give reasons for your choice.

8. Most of the characters approve of slavery. Does this mean we find it hard to like them?

9. How important is the Mississippi in giving unity to the book?

10. What would have been gained or lost if Mark Twain had given other characters' thoughts and feelings, instead of telling the story entirely from Huck's point of view?

EXAMINATION QUESTIONS

1. Many novels centre round a young person growing up. Explain what you have found interesting and attractive about one such story.

2. Does humour in a novel merely amuse us and keep us reading, or can it draw attention to more serious issues? Discuss in relation to your chosen book.

3. The hero or heroine of a novel often has to face some difficult problem or crucial moral choice. Describe the situation confronting one such figure and the way in which he or she comes to a decision.

4. Choose a novel in which the author seems to be attacking some form of social injustice and show how the author draws our attention to this.

5. The changing relationship between characters is an important ingredient in most novels. Show how such a development between two characters is portrayed in any novel you have read.

6. Choose a novel in which the natural setting plays an important part and describe how it affects the lives of the principal characters.

7. Discuss a novel which contains violent episodes; and explain what you think are the author's reasons for introducing these.

8. What means can a writer use to make an unfamiliar background or way of life vivid to readers, without going into long passages of description? Discuss in relation to your chosen book.

9. Most novelists try to make their characters a lifelike mixture of good and bad qualities. Show how this is true of two contrasted characters in any one novel.

10. Why is it that we are amused by episodes or characters in novels that we should not like to be involved with in real life? Discuss this by choosing examples from your chosen novel.

'A really independent person'. How far do you agree with this description of Huck? You should base your answer on *at least two* incidents from the novel.

'We must turn to the women in *The Adventures of Huckleberry Finn* to find trustworthy characters.' Basing your answer on *at least two* women, say how far you agree.

(*Associated Examining Board, June 1982*)

Describe Jim's character. What is his importance in the novel?

'I've never seen anybody but lied,' says Huck at the start of the novel. Basing your answer on *at least two* characters or incidents, say how true his remark is.

(*Associated Examining Board, November 1982*)

FOR THE BEST IN PAPERBACKS, LOOK FOR THE

In every corner of the world, on every subject under the sun, Penguin represents quality and variety – the very best in publishing today.

For complete information about books available from Penguin – including Pelicans, Puffins, Peregrines and Penguin Classics – and how to order them, write to us at the appropriate address below. Please note that for copyright reasons the selection of books varies from country to country.

In the United Kingdom: For a complete list of books available from Penguin in the U.K., please write to *Dept E.P., Penguin Books Ltd, Harmondsworth, Middlesex, UB7 0DA*

In the United States: For a complete list of books available from Penguin in the U.S., please write to *Dept BA, Penguin, 299 Murray Hill Parkway, East Rutherford, New Jersey 07073*

In Canada: For a complete list of books available from Penguin in Canada, please write to *Penguin Books Canada Ltd, 2801 John Street, Markham, Ontario L3R 1B4*

In Australia: For a complete list of books available from Penguin in Australia, please write to the *Marketing Department, Penguin Books Australia Ltd, P.O. Box 257, Ringwood, Victoria 3134*

In New Zealand: For a complete list of books available from Penguin in New Zealand, please write to the *Marketing Department, Penguin Books (NZ) Ltd, Private Bag, Takapuna, Auckland 9*

In India: For a complete list of books available from Penguin, please write to *Penguin Overseas Ltd, 706 Eros Apartments, 56 Nehru Place, New Delhi, 110019*

In Holland: For a complete list of books available from Penguin in Holland, please write to *Penguin Books Nederland B.V., Postbus 195, NL–1380AD Weesp, Netherlands*

In Germany: For a complete list of books available from Penguin, please write to *Penguin Books Ltd, Friedrichstrasse 10 – 12, D–6000 Frankfurt Main 1, Federal Republic of Germany*

In Spain: For a complete list of books available from Penguin in Spain, please write to *Longman Penguin España, Calle San Nicolas 15, E–28013 Madrid, Spain*

FOR THE BEST IN PAPERBACKS, LOOK FOR THE

PENGUIN PASSNOTES

This comprehensive series, designed to help O-level, GCSE and CSE students, includes:

SUBJECTS
Biology
Chemistry
Economics
English Language
Geography
Human Biology
Mathematics
Modern Mathematics
Modern World History
Narrative Poems
Nursing
Physics

SHAKESPEARE
As You Like It
Henry IV, Part I
Henry V
Julius Caesar
Macbeth
The Merchant of Venice
A Midsummer Night's Dream
Romeo and Juliet
Twelfth Night

LITERATURE
Arms and the Man
Cider With Rosie
Great Expectations
Jane Eyre
Kes
Lord of the Flies
A Man for All Seasons
The Mayor of Casterbridge
My Family and Other Animals
Pride and Prejudice
The Prologue to The Canterbury
    Tales
Pygmalion
Saint Joan
She Stoops to Conquer
Silas Marner
To Kill a Mockingbird
War of the Worlds
The Woman in White
Wuthering Heights